# ACADEMY OF
# LEARNING

## Your Complete Preschool Lesson Plan Resource: Volume 3

## © 2015 Breely, Crush & Associates, LLC

*Ver. 112214*

# *Table of Contents*

# Educator Biography

Sharlit Elliott has a B.S. in Elementary Education and Early Childhood from Brigham Young University and has been a teacher for over 15 years working with children ages 3-5. She keeps current on changes in education by attending University classes and conferences several times a year. Besides having raised five children, she has held various leadership positions with the Girl Scouts and the 4-H program. She enjoys gardening, scrapbooking, reading and of course working with children.

# How to Use This Book

This book is designed for a teacher working with children ages 3-5 in a classroom, homeschool or home preschool environment. One of the most important aspects of this series is that it includes fun activities that will enhance their skills. These lessons plans, games and ideas are all for you to use. Don't forget, these are complete lessons and activities that have been designed for compliance with federal and state guidelines for education. We go above and beyond to bring you MORE than what's expected in the public school system.

We will refer to your students as "your children or class". That includes whatever area you are using these lessons for: homeschool or preschool. Our lesson plans include improving student's abilities through activities. The skills we will be working with include: listening skills, music, movement, language and literacy, mathematics, science, fine motor, creative art, sensory, dramatic play, and social skills.

The book is organized by themes which will help you quickly find just the right information. The headings in the book will direct you quickly to large group, small group, and free time activities. It will also provide ideas for field trips.

This book will include the following areas:

### Group Activities/Circle Time

- Music & Movement is used to help develop large muscles in arms and legs. These need to be developed before children can be successful in small muscles activities such as used in writing or cutting with scissors. This area also helps children learn to enjoy music and the basics such as beat, loud/soft and fast/slow.

- Language & Literacy is how we help children learn vocabulary, story order, thinking skills, recall, concepts of the theme, and expressive language.

## Small Group Activities/Table Times

- Math & Cognitive is used to teach numbers, shapes, patterns, sorting, thinking and reasoning skills.

- Fine Motor Skills develop small muscles to be able to draw, write, manipulate small things, to tear, and to cut with scissors.

- Language & Literacy is used to develop skills such as expressive writing, visual memory, matching letters, letter sounds, categorizing items, directional words, and opposites.

- Other creative activities to develop their own uniqueness as an individual.

## Free Time

- Creative arts to draw, build, and develop their imagination.

- Sensory activities are used to learn through exploration and using their senses.

- Dramatic Play & Social Development let children take on different roles, solve problems, find solutions, and develop social interactions.

- Science helps children explore by experimenting, identifying problems, guessing what will happen, checking to see what did happen, questioning how things happened, and developing a plan of what to do next.

- Gross Motor Skills to practice using large and small muscles in fun activities.

- Field Trip Ideas to help children use real places to learn about the world.

Throughout the book we will use the following icons to show the different types of activities:

**MUSIC & MOVEMENT**

**LANGUAGE & LITERACY**

**MATH & COGNITIVE**

**FINE MOTOR SKILLS**

**CREATIVE ARTS**

**SENSORY**

**DRAMATIC PLAY & SOCIAL DEVELOPMENT**

**SCIENCE**

**GROSS MOTOR SKILLS**

**FIELD TRIP IDEAS**

# Introduction to the Units

These lesson plans have been used during the fall with great success. Because of different opinions, policies or religions, sometimes Halloween is not observed in a preschool setting. For example, in the federal Head Start programs, holidays are not observed nor are birthdays. With a mixed group of children, all the lesson plans (except Halloween) can be adjusted, modified or used to replace this particular holiday. In this way, children who do observe the holiday at home are still able to enjoy the "season" and other aspects of the holiday in a fun and safe way. Because all these topics take place in the same season, there is a little overlap from unit to unit, allowing you to pick and choose your favorite activities.

# All About Me

## GROUP ACTIVITIES/CIRCLE TIME

### MUSIC AND MOVEMENT

"I'm a V.I.P." from tape, "I Have A Song For You" by Janeen Brady- Brite Music Enterprises, Inc. Children point to self when saying I'm a V.I.P. in my family. Later have them march in a circle while singing song. It has a good marching beat and using music that sticks with the beat is also fun for them.

"No One Else Can Smile My Smile" from tape, "I Have A Song For You" by Janeen Brady-Brite Music Enterprises, Inc. Have the children smile when singing this song.

"I Love You" from Barney's Favorites Vol. 1. tape By Columbia House.

Children act out the words to song. Example pointing to others when it says "I Love You."

"My Family's Just Right For Me" Favorites Vol. 1. tape. By Columbia House. Prepare pictures of different types of families that go along with the words to show the different types of families sang about. Example - Boy with a Grandmother.

"Shake My Sillies Out" from "Singable Collection - Part 2 More Singable Songs, CD by Raffi. Children love to sing this song while shaking and wiggling their bodies to the words.

"The World Is a Rainbow" from "We All Live Together" Vol. 2. CD By Greg Scelsa. This is a fun song to teach that people come in different colors and when we live in harmony the world is a beautiful rainbow. Children enjoy using hand motions with it. When you sing the word "rainbow" children put their hands up and move them back and forth to create a rainbow. When you say different color names hold your fingers out and point to different fingers while saying the different colors. When you say world make a circle with your arms. When you sing "mix world up", have one arm make circle and the other hand pretends to stir it up. Continue making rainbows with arms and acting out song.

"If You're Happy and You Know It" from "We All Live Together" Vol. 3 CD By Greg Scelsa. The song will lead you to clap your hands, stamp your feet and etc. Children enjoy doing movements to the song. This song helps them to recognize when they are happy.

"Show Me What You Feel" from CD "Kids in Motion" by Greg & Steve. The song directs children to show others how they feel, by directing them to show different emotions like feeling mad and tired. They enjoy acting out these emotions.

"No One Like Me" tape from Macmillan Sing & Learn Program by Newbridge Communications, Inc. This fun song talks about their parts of their body. They enjoy that they are unique and pointing to the part of the body mentioned in the song.

## LANGUAGE AND LITERACY

Doing this theme will give you an opportunity to help children understand that we are all alike in some ways and unique in others. We all have bodies and we all need love. Help them learn that it's ok to be different, but it's not ok to disrespect yourself or others. Reading and discussions of the books you pick from this list or others you have available will help children to understand these ideas. A second important part of this theme is teaching children about their emotions. Children need help in learning to identify their feelings. Point out to children the different facial expressions that help you to know how others are feeling. Be sure to explain that it's ok to be angry, but that it's not ok to hurt others physically or emotionally. If children only learn how to live in a giving and caring way, their preschool experience will have been worth while. It's important that you teach how to share, use their words, trade with others and/or bargain. This unit takes at least two full weeks of class. You can choose to either use the ideas together during two weeks at a time or split it up to do two separate weeks during the year.

We Are All Alike...We Are All Different by Chelten Elementary School Kindergartners, Scholastic Inc. 1991.

The Berenstain Bears by Stan & Jan Berenstain, Scholastic Inc. 1997.

This Is My Family by Gina and Mercer Mayer, Little Golden Books. 1992.

Whoever You Are by Mem Fox, Scholastic Inc. 1997.

When I Was Little: A Four-Year-Old's Memoir of Her Youth by Jamie Lee Curtis, Scholastic Inc. 1998.

Salt in His Shoes: Michael Jordan in Pursuit of a Dream by Deloris Jordan with Roslyn M. Jordan, Simon & Schuster Books For Young Readers. 1963.

Active Minds My Day Consultant Istar Schwager, Ph.D.., Publications International, Ltd. 1994.

Two Eyes, A Nose and A Mouth by Roberta Grobel Intrater, Scholastic Inc. 1995.

The Way I Feel by Janan Cain, Scholastic Inc 2000.

Sometimes I Feel Like a Mouse by Jeanne Modesitt, Scholastic Inc. 1992.

How I Feel by Dave Billman, Landoll, Inc. 1997.

Little Miss Shy by Roger Hargeaves, Ottenheimer Publishers, Inc. 1981.

Little Miss Late by Roger Hargreaves, Price/Stern/Sloan Publishers, Inc. 1984.

Mr. Happy by Roger Hargreaves, Price/Stern/Sloan Publishers, Inc. 1986.

Mr. Busy by Roger Hargreaves, Price/Stern/Sloan Publishers, Inc. 1983.

Dinofours Where's Mommy? by Steve Metzger, Scholastic Inc. 1997.

Dinofours I'm Super Dino! by Steve Metzger, Steve Metzger, Scholastic Inc. 1997.

<u>Make a Face</u> by Henry and Amy Schwartz, Steve Metzger, Scholastic Inc. 1994.

<u>Lost!</u> By David McPhail, Scholastic Inc. 1997.

<u>Feelings</u> by Aliki Brandenberg, Scholastic Inc. 1984.

<u>Alexander and the Terrible, Horrible, No Good, Very Bad Day</u> by Scholastic Inc. 1997. Scholastic Inc. 1989.

<u>Alexander, Who's Not (Do You Hear Me? I Mean It!) Going to Move</u> Scholastic Inc. 1997.

<u>If You're Angry and You Know It!</u> By Cecily Kaiser, Scholastic Inc. 2004.

<u>The Playground Problem</u> by Margaret McNamara, Scholastic Inc. 2004.

<u>Ernie's Little Lie</u> by Dan Elliott, Sesame Street Books & Recordings. 1983.

<u>Don't Hit Me!</u> By Gary Grier, Scholastic Inc. 2004.

<u>I Will Keep Trying</u>! by David Parker, Scholastic Inc. 2005.

<u>I Am Creative!</u> by David Parker, Scholastic Inc. 2005.

<u>I Am a Leader!</u> by David Parker, Scholastic Inc. 2005.

<u>I Can A Share!</u> by David Parker, Scholastic Inc. 2005.

## SMALL GROUP ACTIVITIES/TABLE TIMES

## MATH & COGNITIVE

Trace around an adult foot that is about 12 inches long on dark colored piece of paper. Then cut it out and place the paper on top of 3 or 4 pieces of paper and staple around the edges so that as you cut tracing, you have several sheets cut for patterns. You can laminate them for durability. Cut enough large pieces of butcher paper for each child in the class and the length of the height of children in your class.

When children come to your table, have one child lay on the floor. Show them how to trace around the child's body. Then team them up with a partner and have them take turns tracing each other's body. Next, show them how to use the pattern foot to measure and count how many feet tall they are. It is helpful to have another adult help the children with this project. Ask a parent to see if they could help.

### Container Counting

Children will each have a pail with water in it and a tray with sides on it in front of them. They will each be given a different size of bottle and a scoop (use recycled scoops from laundry detergent). They will also each need a funnel (buy sets of funnels at the Dollar Store). Children will guess how many scoops of water it will take to fill their bottle. Then they will put their bottle on the tray and put their funnel into it. Next they will carefully scoop water from the pail and pour it into the bottle as they count the number of scoops it will take. They will see how close their guesses came to the real count. This helps them with estimation skills and develops their self confidence.

### Lid Puzzle

Save various empty and washed containers such as - cottage cheese carton with lid, peanut butter jar with lid, water bottles and juice containers with lids of various sizes, pizza sauce the other jars, oatmeal box with lid, baby wipe box with lid, baby jars with lids, ice cream pails with lids, small yogurt containers with lids, and any other safe containers.

Set the items out on the table with the lids off and ask the children to match up the container with its lid. They can also see which containers will fit inside others. This exercise helps them develop thinking skills which helps them to learn how to use parts to make things whole and gives them a cognitive base to build on. This type of "hands on" activity helps them to develop the more abstract skill they will need later.

### Plastic Boxes

The boxes used in the "Get Acquainted Theme" (volume 1) activity can be used today in a different way. Get out three or four boxes and place all their contents on the table. Have children match the items that are the same type of thing. Like all the close pins or button could be put in their own area of the table. Next have them sort within their area the different colors, shapes or sizes. They can also look for things like all the same size button with the same number of holes in the buttons. Another great "hands on" activity to get them thinking and noticing difference and similarities

## Sink Float

Teacher will collect various items from around the room such as – a screw, crayons, cotton balls, craft sticks, straws, pipe cleaners, feathers, plastic spoons, foil, small pieces of paper, pencils, small toy cars, plastic small toys, wood blocks, plant leaves, or anything else you can think of that will fit into a dish pan. Assemble your items and have the children guess before they take turns placing each item into the water.

Ask them, "What do you think will happen? Do you think it will sink or float?" After each item has been placed into the pail of water ask, "Why do you think it sunk or floated?" Place all the items that floated or sunk in different areas that have the word sink or float written in the corresponding area. As more of the items sink or float have them look at the areas of separated items and ask them to look for things in that area that may be alike in some way. Continue until all the items have been used. Help the children see some of the reasons why an item may have sunk or may have floated. Do this activity another day using different items to help them learn to see the similarities and difference in things.

## Magnets

Prepare items similar to the items used in the sink or float activity. Also include many different things that a magnet will attract like - nails, paper clips, fingernail files, some scissors, bobby pins, and other small metal items. Mix the items that will be attracted by a magnetic wand or other strong magnet with the items that will not me attracted by the magnet.

Children will come to the table and guess what will happen if the magnet touches any item. Have areas with the word "attracts" and "will not attract" as in activity of "sink & float". Children will take turns picking an object to see if it will attract. They will tell their guess and then they will test it by using the magnet. Next they will place it the marked areas of attracts or will not attract. Ask children after a number of objects are in the different areas if they can see things that are similar to the ones placed in the same groups. Continue until all the objects have been used. Help children to see similarities and differences in the items in each group. Do this another day and see if they will start to guess correctly next time.

## Pattern Chain

Use a paper cutter to cut colored construction paper into 1 ½ inch by 9 inch lengths. Use only two or three different colors. Explain to the children that they will be making a pattern. If it is their first time use only two colors and later when they understand it they can use up to four colors.

Make a circle (chain) with one of the strips by gluing the over-lapped ends or by stapling the over-lapped ends. Next take a different color and put the strip through the first circle and overlap its ends and glue or staple together to form another connecting circle. Continue in this manner using the first color again and then the second color again. Explain to the children that this makes a pattern of two colors. Tell them to choose a color and make a circle the same way as you did. Now they will choose their second color and put it through the first circle as you showed them to form another circle. Continue by adding 1st and 2nd colors rotating them. If they don't get it this time, you can use this for other patterning on other days. Hang the colorful chains up to decorate the room.

**Eye Graph**

Make large eyes of brown, blue and green. See pattern below Make enough for your class. Prepare a poster board with three columns. Put a different color of eye at the top of each column. Have a small mirror so that children can look at their eyes in it. Ask them to decide it their eyes look like they are blue, green or brown. Then they will pick up a correspondent color of an eye and place it in the column under that color of eye. This group of children at your table could be a little larger than your regular size group. After everyone in the group has placed their eye color on the poster have them look to see which column is longest and which is shortest and which if any is in between. Then count together each column of eye color and write that number on the piece of paper. Children will tell which color of eyes had the most in their group. Talk about that they all have eyes and that they all see with them. You can do this activity another day using hair color.

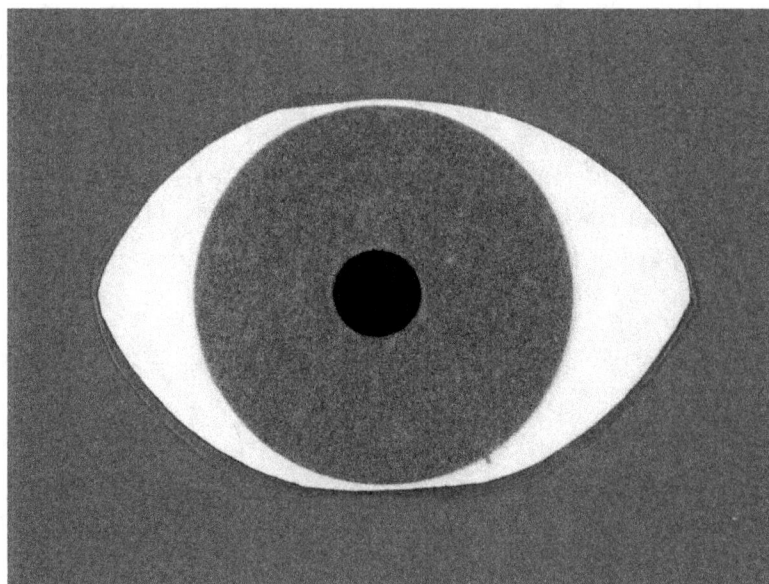

**Weight**

Ask parent to write down their child's weight when he/she was born. Bring a scale to school. Prepare a paper with a simple picture of a baby on it. Also include a line where each child can write their name on it. The paper should also have a place to record the child's newborn weight and a place for their present weight along with the date.

Children come to the table and receive the prepared piece of paper and a pencil to write their name on the page. Next, show the children the numerals 1-10. Ask each child to guess a number from 1-10 that they think may have weighted when they were a tiny new baby. Then the children will listen as the teacher reads to them what their parent said that they weight. The teacher will point at the number that corresponds with that number. Then show them the place where they will write that number with help, if needed.

The children will take turns on the scale to see how much they weigh now. Help them record the weight and the date. This will help make numerals more meaningful to them. Children can draw at the bottom of their page how they look today. Be sure and add this page to a file for them to get back at the end of the year.

## FINE MOTOR SKILLS

**My Home**

Have different colors of construction paper available for the children, crayons, markers and scissors. Children will choose a color of paper to make a house. Instruct children to fold their paper in half in either direction depending how they want it to look. It can be made either tall or wide. Then have the children cut the top of the corners off making a rectangle shape cut. This will be the roof. Now they will draw widows and then a door on the front of their home. Next they will open the folded house and create what they think in should look like inside the home. They could draw beds, tables, their family or whatever they want. See example.

### Crown

Make a simple crown pattern on colored or plain construction paper. Then the children or teacher will trace around it or have the children trace around it on the colored paper of their choosing. Now the children will cut out the crown. Teacher will set out various small items for children to collage on their crown. These items can then be glued on by the children. These are some of the items that can be used - colored macaroni, small beads, colored sequins, paste jewels and/or foam cut outs. Then, staple an extra length of paper on each end so that it will fit around the child's head forming a crown. Let it dry and then they can wear it.

### Family Shield

Make a shield pattern such as the example below. Children will use the pattern to trace their own shield on construction paper. Then they will cut the shield out with small children's scissors. Next, ask them to think about what their family is like. Example they have two brothers, they all have brown hair, they like cookies, they love each other.

Now on their shield they will draw the things that they thought about that describes their family. Be sure that you have the crayons and/or markers ready. Also, the children will write their names on the top of their shields. Later at the circle time, let them take turns showing and telling about their family shield.

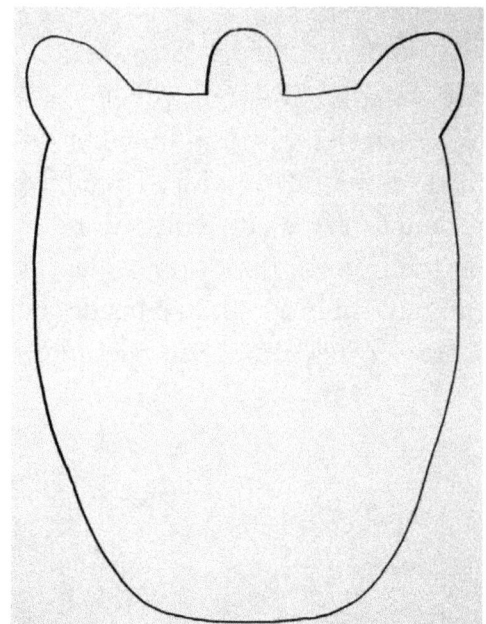

## Paper Plate

In this activity gather pictures of different foods from magazines and newspaper advertisements. Also have scissors, glue and paper plates ready for children's use. Children will look through the different foods and will find foods that they like to eat. They will cut out the foods that they like and glue those pictures on to their plate. Then they will tell those at the table what the foods are that they like. They will also listen to the others at the table to hear what foods they like and listen to see if the foods are the same or different than the ones that they like.

## Fingerprints

Teacher will have washable ink pads and pieces of paper ready for this activity. Children will take turns putting each finger of one or both hands onto the ink pad and then on to their paper to make prints of their fingers. Then they will look as their prints with a magnifying glass. Next they will look to see the different prints that each finger made. Tell them that no two people's fingerprints are exactly the same, but that we all have fingerprints. Now have them continue to make prints to create a picture. They can also use makers with their prints to make different things.

## Finger-painting

Prepare two small boxes of instant pudding following direction on the boxes. Use chocolate, butter-scotch, or other dark colored pudding flavors. Take it out of the fridge a little before time you will use it, so that it won't be too cold. Give each child a small sample of each pudding to taste. Put out a sheet of the glossy finger-paint paper for each child. Then put a scoop of their chosen pudding on their piece of paper. They will make lines and drawings on the paper. Before the children leave, have them tell you which pudding that they liked best. Have the children count with you the number of children that choose each type of pudding. Then ask which pudding did more of the children choose? Discuss the idea that it's ok if we don't all like the same things.

## Paper Dolls

Use a large pattern of a paper doll like example. Cut out enough construction paper so that each child can pick a skin color of their choosing. Have various pieces of cloth material in checks, solids and different prints. Also, have pieces of ribbon, yarn in hair colors and felt in eye colors and mouth colors.

Children will use scissors and glue to create a doll to look like themselves by gluing on pieces of felt for eyes and mouth and yarn for hair. The other materials will be used to

put clothing on the doll. Point out that we all have different colors of eyes put that we all have so we can all see.

## Glitter Names

Print each child's first name across a piece of poster board to be able to have each letter 2 inches tall. Cut the poster board an inch or two below their printed name in a straight line. Now give each child a small glue bottle to trace each printed letter in their name. Then they will sprinkle glitter on the glue and dump off the excess glitter on to a tray. When their names are dry, they can take them home or leave at school for a few days to display.

## Hand Print Card

Fold a piece of card stock in half to create a card. Have poster paint mixed with dish soap in a small flat bakery foam tray for children to dip their hand into mixture. Assemble markers or crayons.

Children will draw inside the folded card stock something that they are thankful to their family for. Example - for the love in our home, how we help each other, our food. They will dictate to you what their drawing represents and you will write what they said inside their card.

Next they will close their card and dip their hand into the paint. Now they will press their hand on to the front of their card. When it is dry, send home this special card to their family.

## LANGUAGE AND LITERACY

## People Cards

Make cards of people doing various activities. Look through magazines for people doing things like gardening, eating, exercising, swimming, and other actions. Then cut out the pictures and mount them on card stock.

Show the children the pictures one at a time. Ask children one at a time what the people are doing in the pictures. Try to help them add "ing" to their words like-swimming instead of swim. This activity will help them with their vocabulary. Continue until all the cards have been used. Afterwards you can ask children which pictures they liked best and why they liked the picture.

## Body Parts

Teacher prepares a picture by drawing or finding a picture of a child's body with clothes on. Mount this picture on poster board. Then, show the picture to children. Teacher will point to a part of the body like the knee and children will take turns answering the question what is the name of that body part. This activity continues until teacher has pointed to all the body parts like ear, mouth, nose, ankle, back and etc. Then the children will take turns pointing to different body parts and having other children name them. Many children do not know some of the simple body part names like waist, wrist, eyebrow, and eye lashes. This will help them increase their vocabulary.

## Interview

Use a pretend microphone made from an empty paper towel roll. Sometimes in dollar stores you can buy a pretend microphone that echoes the voice when spoken into them. From a prepared list, ask children one at a time things like - what is your favorite color, what do you like to eat, how old are you and how many people are in your family. Encourage children to be good listeners and to remember one thing the child said. After each child's interview ask the other children to name one thing that the child said about their self. Encourage them to remember and name something different than the last child said.

## Clothing Props

Ask parents for hats and other clothing that children could relate the props to different things that people do. Such as a baker's hat, a tutu, a baton, a cowboy hat, a sailors hat, a clown hat and a construction worker's hat. If you don't get the props you want try a thrift store.

Children will take turns picking a prop and wearing or holding it. Then they will say how the prop made them feel. They might say they felt silly or funny wearing it the clown's hat. Play continues until all the children have had a turn. Talk with the children about different kinds of feeling and explain to them that we all have different types of feelings.

## Feeling Puppets

Teacher explains to children that we all have many different feeling. Then give out a finger puppet for each child to wear. Explain to them that the faces on the puppets are like people's faces. They help us know how the person is feeling. Talk about each finger puppet's facial expression and talk about how they think that person may be feeling.

Now have children take turns putting on the different finger puppets. They will use their voices and words like that puppet would use with that emotion. This will help children with their expressive language skills. See puppets.

## Role Play

After reviewing the class rule of "mind and be kind," use puppets to role play emotions sad, mad and happy.

Teacher will have a puppet on each hand. One puppet will be playing with (holding) a small toy. The other puppet will come up and grab the toy away. The other puppet will hit the one who took the toy away. Then we will stop and talk about mad. That it's ok to be mad, but that it's not ok to hit. Then ask what the person could do or say. Continue discussion until children say different words that the puppet could say or do. Example - tell the person, "That makes be mad when you take my toy away" or "I had that first." Then talk about what the other person could do instead of grabbing the toy. Example - say, "Can I have a turn with when you are finished?" or "Can I play with the toy with you?" Play continues with children taking turns in pairs using one puppet each. Children will do the talking and actions with a little guiding by teacher. Summarize the activity by identifying how both children can be happy.

## Health Objects

Collect objects that help us stay clean and healthy such as - comb, toothbrush, toothpaste, bar of soap, dental floss, wash cloth, towel, shampoo, nail brush, and a file. In this activity the teacher will place the objects on the table. The children will take turn selecting the appropriate item after being told the function of the object. Example - Which one do we clean our hair with? Child picks shampoo. When finished with objects tell them that they can do many things for their self now that they are bigger. Read to them <u>When I Get Bigger</u>, by Mercer Mayer and have them look for things that they can do.

## Counting Body Parts

As a group, at the table have the children find different body parts and count them. The teacher might say fingernails and everyone would find their fingernails and count them. Then a child would say another body part like knees and they would all find theirs and count them. Play continues until each child has at least one turn. Children cannot say the same thing that someone else has said. The teacher may help the child it needed. It would be fun to have mirrors for them to use, if someone said teeth, so that like could see them to count. This will increase their body awareness and their vocabulary.

## Simon Says

Play Simon says. "Simon says, "Skip around the table being happy." Simon says, "Stop." Simon says, "Stomp around the table being angry." Simon says, "Stop." Continue using different emotions. Some examples are - walk very slowly around table being sad, hop around table being silly, tip toeing around table being scared, and walk while stretching around the table being sleepy. Don't do many tricks so that they will stay focused on the feeling.

## FREE TIME

**CREATIVE ARTS**

Set out trays and put shaving cream on them. Let the children create pictures using their fingers to make the designs. Have a pail of warm water nearby, to wash the shaving cream off before it gets all over the sink handles.

Put large pieces of paper on the easel and then different colors of bingo markers on the trays for children to use. Children can make dots into many different designs. Another day set out the watercolors with paper and let them create what ever they want.

## SENSORY

Put small zip lock bags with play dough in them. Tell the children to replace the dough into the bag when they are finished so that it does not dry out. They can create with the dough and use craft sticks to help them create. This activity helps them to strengthen fingers and to enjoy different textures.

Fill sensory tub half full of warm water with bio water coloring. If not available use a little food coloring to color the water. Then put in scoops and water/sand mills. You can find these in the summer months in the outdoors toy departments. The bio color is found in many school supply stores or online.

## DRAMATIC PLAY & SOCIAL DEVELOPMENT

Collect old fashioned dress items that grandma and grandpa used to wear such as long skirts, dresses and suits. Buy from a Thrift Store or get parents to contribute clothing and shoes. These clothing and shoes many have belonged to children a few years older. The size of clothing needs to be only a few sizes larger so that it will fit them over their own clothing. You can make simple skirts using elastic for the waist. They enjoy the high heels and dad's dress shoes as well. Old jewelry and ties add to their wardrobe fun.

## SCIENCE

Display a rock collection with labels on the rocks or by them. Also have magnifier glass so that the children can examine them closely. You can buy small rocks at local earth museums or start your own collection. Buy or check out a picture book on rocks and minerals from the library. Put books from the library on the science table with the rocks. Posters on rocks are also available at school supply stores.

## GROSS MOTOR SKILLS

### Follow the Leader

Play follow the leader by telling the children to do what you are doing. Tell them that they will need to watch and listen closely because the actions will keep changing. Teacher will do this game for the first few times. Then when they are ready you can have them take turns being the leader. You can do this inside if you do less active motor like flying like a bird and walking like an elephant. More active motor should be done outside.

To play, teacher says and demonstrates what children are to do. Examples - Hopping with two feet, then change to hopping with right foot and then left foot, next skipping and walking side ways.

### Bean Bag Toss

Tell children that they are going to toss bean bag to each other and catch them. Divide the class into two groups. Make two lines and have the lines parallel to each other about three feet apart. Assign the children the person across from them to be their partner. Tell children that when the music starts they will throw the bean bag to their partner and their partner will try and catch it. Tell them not to throw the bean bag hard only soft. Tell them that when the music stops they will freeze (hold perfectly still).

Now pass out the bean bags to one line of children. Start the music and then when they have thrown it for 3 or 4 minutes stop the music and remind them to freeze. Give them more instructions if needed at this time and start the music again. Stop the game before they get tired so that they will want to play the game another day.

### Pass the Ball

Have the children sit in a circle either outside or inside. Tell them that they will be playing a game of pass the ball. Demonstrate how to pass the ball around the circle without stopping the ball. Then tell the children that when they play the game you will say pass the ball when you want them to start and freeze when they should stop passing the ball. The person who has the ball when the teacher says stop tells something about himself/herself. Give them some examples such as - I'm four years old, I like to play with cars/ dolls, my favorite colors are and etc.

Now begin the game. It is better not to use music this time, so that the game does not last too long. This way the teacher can say freeze when she/he wants that particular child to have a turn and still have time for each child to have a turn.

**FIELD TRIP IDEAS**

Go on a walking field trip to collect rocks or if possible arrange for transportation to a nearby canyon, dry river bed or dessert if they are close.

Make sure you get permission notes from parents, even if it's close by. Arrange for as many parents as you can to go with you. This way it is safer and more children get one on one attention. Give each of the children an empty egg carton to collect their rocks in and to use to display their rocks. Make sure that their name is on the top of their box.

When you get back have the children with the adults compare their rocks to the displayed collection and to the pictures in the books. See if any of the look familiar. Children can keep their collection for all to look at and they can take them home.

Go to a rock or mineral show or visit an earth science museum. Many colleges also have rocks and minerals in their geology department and they may allow you to visit them and tell the children about the rocks and mineral and let them handle them. Be sure once again to get the permission notes and as many parents as possible to go with you.  If you do not have transportation available check with local college. Sometimes they will send someone out to your school to show the rocks and talk to the children about them or they many let you check out some of the rocks.

## Wheat & Grains

**GROUP ACTIVITIES/CIRCLE TIME**

**MUSIC AND MOVEMENT**

Sing the Peanut Butter Song with the children. This is a fun song that is easy to learn.

**"Peanut Butter"** Music and Lyrics Traditional

First you take the peanuts and you crunch' em,

you crunch'em, you crunch'em, crunch'em, crunch them.

Chorus: Peanut, peanut butter –jelly

Then you take the peanuts and you smash'em,

you smash'em, you smash'em, smash'em, smash them.

Chorus: Peanut, peanut butter –jelly

Then you take the peanuts and you mix'em,

you mix'em, you mix'em, mix'em, mix them.

Chorus: Peanut, peanut butter – jelly

Then you take the grapes and you squish'em,

you squish'em, you squish'em, squish'em, squish them.

Chorus: Peanut, peanut butter –jelly

Then you take the grapes and you stir'em,

you stir'em, you stir'em, stir'em, stir them.

Chorus: Peanut, peanut butter – jelly

Now you take a big slice of bread with peanut butter

and you spread it, you spread it, you spread it, spread it, spread it.

Chorus: Peanut, peanut butter – jelly

Then you take the jelly and you spread it, you spread it,

you spread it, spread it, spread it.

Chorus: Peanut, peanut butter – jelly

Then you take your big sandwich and you bite it, you bite it,

you bite it, bite it, bite it.

Chorus: Peanut, peanut butter – jelly

MMMM -- that was good!

Have the children act out the verse words in the song using hand movements. For example when it comes to the squishing movement, have them rub their palms together while squeezing them together. In the chorus, have them shake their hands down low when they say "peanut, peanut butter" then a small pause until they throw their hands up in the air and say "jelly".

Another great song to sing is Hot Cross Buns, which is an old English street song that peddlers used to sing to attract customers to buy their wares.

**Hot Cross Buns** - Author unknown

Hot cross buns,

hot cross buns,

One a penny, two a penny,

hot cross buns.


If you have no daughters,

feed them to your sons,

One a penny, two a penny,

Hot cross buns.

The following is a list of additional songs that you can play and sing with this unit:

"Oats and Beans and Barley" found in Baby Beluga - by Raffi

"Biscuits in the Oven" found in Baby Beluga - by Raffi

"Muffin Man" found in We All Live Together Volume 2 - by Greg Scelsa

"Popcorn" found in We All Live Together Volume 2 - by Greg Scelsa

"Who Stole the Cookies From the Cookie Jar?" found in Wee Sing - Grandpa's Magical Toys

"Sandwiches" found in Fred Penner Collections by Fred Penner

"Pizza Hut" found in Just For Fun – by Dr. Jean

"On Top of Spaghetti" music, words and finger play found in <u>Eye Winker Tom Tinker Chin Chopper</u> by Tom Glazer

"Pat-A-Cake" music, words and finger play found in <u>Eye Winker Tom Tinker Chin Chopper</u> by Tom Glazer

You can buy these songs on CD or cassette. Some are now even offered on the internet for download. For example, at www.fredpenner.com you can listen to the songs for free. We recommend buying used CDs or cassettes through a company online such as www.abebooks.com or www.half.com where you can find these relatively easy and inexpensively.

## LANGUAGE AND LITERACY

These are some books that will help children learn that grains are used in many foods we eat. It is important to especially point out the many things that are made with wheat.

<u>Pancakes For Breakfast</u> by Tomie DePAOLA

<u>Noisy Breakfast</u> by Ellen Blonder

<u>Hi, Pizza Man</u> by Virginia Walter

<u>On Top of Spaghetti</u> by Tom Glazer

<u>Bread and Jam</u> for Frances by Russell Hoban

<u>Curious George Makes Pancakes</u> by Margret & H. A. Rey

<u>Froggy Bakes A Cake</u> by Jonathan London

<u>If You Give A Pig A Pancake</u> by Laura Numeroff

<u>If You Give A Moose A Muffin</u> by Laura Joffe Numeroff

<u>If You Give A Mouse A Cookie</u> by Laura Joffe Numeroff

<u>Pancakes, Pancakes!</u> By Eric Carle

<u>Who Took the Cookies from the Cookie Jar?</u> By Bonnie Lass & Philemon Sturges

<u>I Know an Old Lady Who Swallowed a Pie</u> by Allison Jackson

The Little Red Hen an old Folktale retold by many authors


By reading books to children each day you help them develop a rich vocabulary. It will also help them learn to express themselves if you give them lots of opportunities to answer open ended questions while reading or at the end of the story. An open ended question has no wrong or right answer. It gives them a chance to tell what they are thinking or feeling about the book. An example of an open ended question that you could ask would be, "what was your favorite part of the story?" You could also ask how they felt when you reached different parts in the story.

Another reason to read to children is to help them learn to listen for what happened in the book or what the author wanted you to learn. This is an example of a fun way to accomplish this goal. To teach children to learn to listen for information use the book Froggy Bakes a Cake. Then, assemble the items Froggy used to make his cake and place them in a bag or a box.

You could use real eggs or plastic ones, a small cup or bag of flour, a stick of butter, a tin of baking powder, a container of salt, chocolate candies, a small container of milk, a small bag of sugar, and a yellow bowl and a spoon to stir. Take the items out one at a time from the container. Have the children say the name of each item as you show them one by one. Then ask them to listen to the story and try to remember how each item was used, such as the eggs cracked and some fell on the floor.

Next, read the story while pointing out the pictures. Then have the children take turns telling the class what they remembered about each item. For example, he cracked seven eggs or he used the whole box or baking powder. Be sure and give each child a positive response for their comments. For example, wow, you remembered how the stick of butter fell on the floor.

You will be surprised how much they can learn to remember, but only when they have been taught to look and listen.

The story of The Little Red Hen is a fun one to read with the children. They make the animal noises as the hen ask each animal to help with the work. For example, the children bark and say "Not I said the dog." They will enjoy hearing this simple story again and again. You could purchase flannel figures for this story from a flannel board company or make your own figures on paper. Then have the pictures laminated and glue a magnet strip on the back so they can stick to a metal cookie sheet or metal board. Now they can tell the story to others. Because some cookie sheets are aluminum, magnets will not stick so we sure beforehand what type of cookie sheet you plan to use. Another alternative to this is some stores like Ikea offer a metal version of a white board. These are magnetic but also work with dry erase markers. At a cost of under $20 this may be something you can use again and again.

## SMALL GROUP ACTIVITIES/TABLE TIMES

### MATH & COGNITIVE

Cooking involves math (counting & measuring), science (seeing the product change from a liquid to a solid and also change its size), as well as developing thinking skills (predicting what will happen next). Cooking also helps children develop their self-esteem.

When cooking with children, do the activity at the very start of their class, so you have time to complete activity and have time for them to sample the food.

### Rolls or Small Loaves of Bread

**Before Starting assemble the following:** flour, sugar, salt, yeast, spray oil, warm water, measuring cups and measuring spoons, hot pads, cookie sheets or small loaf pans, masking tape, waterproof pen, plastic wrap, clean table, oven, butter or margarine, copy the recipe on a large sheet of paper.

### Small Loaves

To make small loaves of bread prepare surfaces by using spray oil on small loaf pans. This helps keep loaves from sticking. Use masking tape with each child's name and place it on outside of their loaf tin.

### Rolls

To make rolls use cookie sheets. Cover cookie sheets with foil. Then use masking tape to section them off and write on the masking tape the square that each child will place their roll. Then spray oil on the foil to keep from sticking. See example.

**Prepare children** by having them wash their hands and tell them not to wipe noses or put fingers in their mouths, so that the dough will stay clean. Tell the children that they will be taking turns putting in the ingredients.

Now, show them the recipe. Explain that it's important to know how to read and count so that the bread turns out correct.

Have children look at and smell each of the ingredients while making the dough. Make sure to place special emphasis on telling them about the yeast. Explain to them it is a tiny plant that can grow to make the dough rise. Have them watch it as it grows while adding the other ingredients.

Also show them different types of measuring cups and spoons. Tell them how many will make one cup. For example, "It takes 2 of the ½ cups to make 1 whole cup." Explain to them that these measures look like cups, so we call them measuring cups. Show measuring spoon and tell them that they look like spoons, so we call them measuring spoons. Show them that it takes 4 of the 1/4 Tsp. to make 1 Tb.

**Recipe for the Dough for Rolls and Loaves**

Put 1 Tb. of yeast on top of 1/4 C. warm water and sprinkle ½ Tsp. sugar on yeast. Set this aside.

Combine in bread mixer (or in a large bowl): 1/3 C. cooking oil, 1/3 C. sugar, 1 Tb. salt, and 2 ½ C. warm water.

Add 3 ½ C. flour while mixer is working (or while stirring the ingredients). Mix thoroughly.

Then add the yeast mixture. Add 1 ½ C. more flour on top of yeast and mix for 5 minutes in bread mixer (or by hand until mixed thoroughly). Next sprinkle 1 ½ to 2 ½ cups more flour. The dough will cling together and come away from the sides of the bowl. Keep adding a little flour at a time until the dough does come away from the sides of the bowl completely.

**For Rolls:** Put about a third of a cup of flour in front of each child on a clean table. Have the children spread the flour all over their hands. Demonstrate kneading the dough by flouring your hands, taking a 2 to 3 inch ball of dough and dropping it on your flour. Roll it in the flour so it won't be too sticky. Then use one hand to flatten dough. Next fold it in half and push it down with the tips of your figures. Repeat flattening and fold it several more times.

Then give each child their dough to work on as you have shown them. If their hands get sticky have them put more flour on them and roll the dough off their hands. When they are tired of kneading the dough have them form a ball with their dough.

Next, they will place it on a prepared cookie sheet to rise. Teacher sprays plastic wrap with spray oil and then puts the oil side down over all the rolls on the cookie sheet.

**For Small Loaves:** Use enough dough that would fill the small pans half full. Proceed as with rolls, but have them kneed at least 10 times. Then have them flatten the dough on the table. Next roll it up longwise like a hot dog and place it in their pans with the seam down. Now, spray the plastic wrap with cooking oil and place it over the loaf tins with the oil side down on the loaves.

When the loaves have doubled in size, remove the plastic wrap and place them in a preheated oven at 350 degrees for about 15 minutes. Watch for them to be a light, golden brown color. Oven temperatures can vary so keep an eye on them you desired color and doneness.

Place them on a cooling rack when done and serve them warm with butter.

**Approximate amounts:** This will make 32 rolls or 6 of the 2x5 small pans.

## Make Muffins

If you do not want to make bread, but still would like to cook with the children, use a muffin mix. Make a poster of the directions on the box for children to follow. Assemble all of the ingredients. Have the children count the amounts of ingredients to put in. For example: 2 cups of water. Make sure the table is clean and that the children have washed their hands before starting. Then, have the children help measure and put in the ingredients. Let them have a chance to mix the ingredients using a spoon. Lastly, have them put cup cake liner papers in the muffin pan and put the batter into them. After cooking the muffins, let the children sample their work by eating them.

## Painting Toast

This is a fun activity that kids love. First assemble: white bread, canned milk, a can opener for the canned milk, food coloring, small new brushes or special cooking ones, several small bowls and a toaster. You can choose to use either evaporated milk which makes a thinner paint or condensed milk which will make the paint pudding like. I generally use the evaporated milk, but either will work.

First mix the canned milk with the food color. Add enough coloring to achieve a dark color. You can also have them mix two colors together and see if they can predict what new color it will make.

Mix several different colors in separate small bowls. Then have the children dip their brush into the colors to paint onto the bread. When they are through with their design, ask them what they think will happen when they put them into the toaster.

Next, place the bread into the toaster. Be sure and keep the children safe from getting burned by a hot toaster. Also, make sure that the toaster is turned to a light shade to cook.

When the toast pops up have them tell you if the toast looks like they thought it would. Last of all have them spread butter on it and eat it!

## Pancake Counters

Using brown or tan paper and a lid from a cottage or similar size lid trace around it to form the circle pancake shapes. You can also use felt, foam or a place mat to make pancakes from. Then, cut out ten pancakes or more. Label each pancake with a number 1-10 or higher. If you used paper to make them, be sure to laminate them now. The other materials will not need to be laminated. Have the children count and arrange the

numbers in their correct order with you. When first teaching them their numbers, only use 1-5. After doing this several times, mix up the numbered pancakes and have the children take turns putting them in correct number order. They can have teacher or other children help them if needed. Also be sure and have them say the numbers as they arrange them. Later you can have them go to 10 of higher.

## Cookie Shape Fun

Use smaller lid from margarine tub or yogurt container to trace around. You can use various materials to make the cookie shapes like the ones listed in the "pancake turners".

After making the cookie shapes, place one shape on each of the cookies. Use shapes like a square, triangle, rectangle, diamond, heart, star, crescent, or circles. You can either trace shapes on colored paper and glue them on or use sticker shapes to place on the cookies. Make as many sets of the shapes as you want.

Then you will turn the shape side down on the table. Children will take turns picking a cookie. They will turn it over and tell you the name of the shape on the cookie. Play continues until all of the shapes have been named.

You can also play this game another way for beginners. Place three of each of the shape cookies on the table face up. Have four or five of the each of the same shape cookie you are working on mixed up in a pile. Then have the children take turns drawing a card and match it to one of the cookies that are across the top of the table. Teacher and children will say the shape name together. Continue to play until all of the cookies have been matched up.

## Sprouting Seeds

Soak wheat grains and or beans in warm water for an hour. Talk about how the wheat that grew in the story of <u>The Little Red Hen</u>. Ask them what they think will happen if they put the seeds in water.

Later in the day after the seeds have soaked have the children put some seeds into their own small zip lock bag and zip it closed. Put a damp folded paper towel into some of them and no water in others. Tape the bags with their names on them onto a windowpane where the sun shines in.

Use a prepared small clipboard for each of the children to draw how the seeds looked when they placed them in the bag and record how the seeds changes using other drawings. Talk about what happens. If some have too much water and go moldy, ask the children what would happen if less water was in their towel.

If they sprouted and grew talk about what helped the seed to grow. Plant some and place them in the dark and ask what they think will happen. Children will develop thinking skills and increasing their vocabulary while doing this project. You can add soil to increase the experience of what will happen.

To make a small clipboard, cut rectangle pieces of cardboard from boxes and cut papers the same size. Then staple several pages of papers to the cardboard and attach a piece of yarn tied to a pencil for the children to use to record their drawings. They can real scientists now.

## Breadsticks

Use real breadsticks for this activity. Cut the breadsticks into four different sizes. Each child will arrange their bread sticks from longest to shortest and then from shortest to longest. When they put them into the correct order and say how they have arranged them, they can eat them. You can also use pieces of other grain things such as spaghetti or other noodles, but sure that the items used are visibly different in sizes.

## Pasta Sort

Buy a variety of different shapes of pasta and have children sort it into groups that are alike. Then have them count how many are in each group. If you don't want them to have too many check the amounts of each type so it won't be too many to count. For example, have 10 bowtie pasta, 7 macaroni, 8 large shells, and 4 spiral type. Next have them put the different types of pasta each in their own line. As you count them write down how many are in each type. When they have counted each type, have they tell you which type there is more of and which type have less. You can also use ordinal counting, such as this is the 1st group, the 2nd group, the 4th group and the 5th group.

## Bread Counting

Use the examples below to make your own bread people. You can make as many of these pages based on your time and the counting ability of the children. Copy enough for each child.

Next use crackers, small bread cut outs, or uncooked macaroni as counters to glue onto the long rectangles. They will glue only the amount of counters that represents the numbers on the bread people's faces.

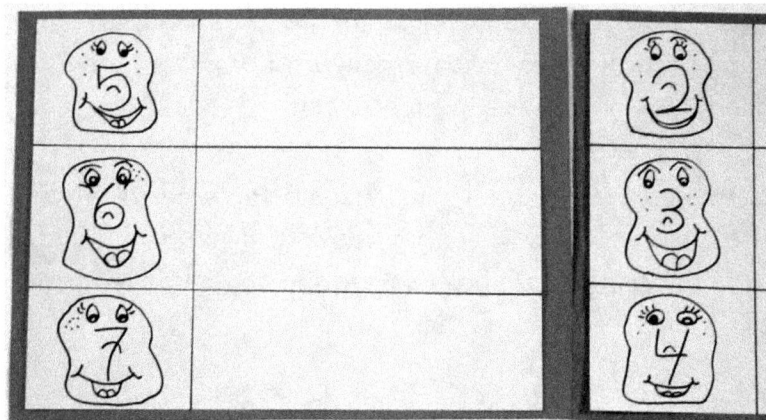

## FINE MOTOR SKILLS

### Waffles

Prepare or copy a waffle pattern. Tell children that they will be drawing a waffle. Have the children carefully connect the 1 dot to the 2 dot by using their rulers and pressing against it with their pencil. Then connect the 2 dot to the 3 dot and then to the 4 dot. Their waffle is almost complete. Let them add water colors over it for brown syrup or other colors for jam. This skill helps to develop eye-hand coordination. Use pattern like one to the right.

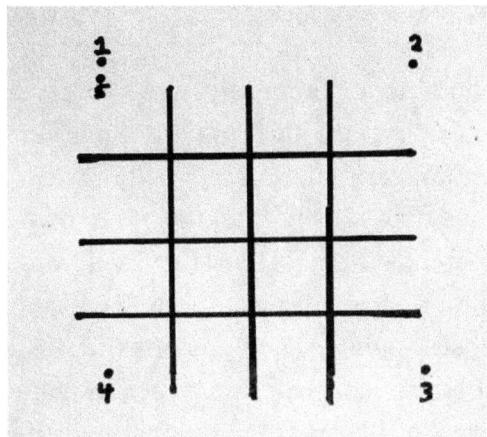

### Cake or Cupcake

On white card stock paper draw a cupcake or cake like the one below. Tell the children that they will spread the pretend icing on them. Be sure and to tell that it isn't real icing and what's made out of so they will not eat it. Use plastic knives to spread it or wood craft sticks (popsicle).

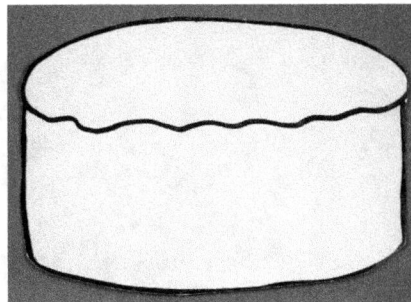

Make the pretend icing by squirting shaving cream into a bowl. Then add white school glue to it along with food coloring in whatever shade that you would like. The proportions are about 2 cups sprayed shaving cream to about ½ school glue and 1 to 2 tsp. food coloring. You can have them add real candles or cut colored pipe cleaners. It will dry puffy. This is also an eye-hand coordination skill.

### Cupcake or Cinnamon Roll

Copy or draw the cupcake and/or the cinnamon roll below on to light tan paper. Children will use white poster paint with a paint brush to draw icing on them and then they will sprinkle glitter on to the paint while it is still wet. They will look good enough to eat and will be a fun eye-hand coordination skill.

## Pizza

Use large lids from cottage cheese container or other large ones to have children trace around with a marker on tan construction paper. Tell them that they will be making their own pretend pizza. Then they will cut the crust (circle) out. Now have red poster paint (sauce) and paint brushes so they can add their sauce. Next have various colors of construction paper to make pineapple, peppers, olives, ham or whatever they like on their pizza. They can tear the paper into the shapes they want or use scissors to cut it. Also, have yellow yarn (cheese) available for them to use. If the sauce is still wet the things will stick on, but if it isn't holding they can glue it on. Their pizzas will have just what they want on them and they will have used cutting, tearing and collage to strengthen their fingers. See example.

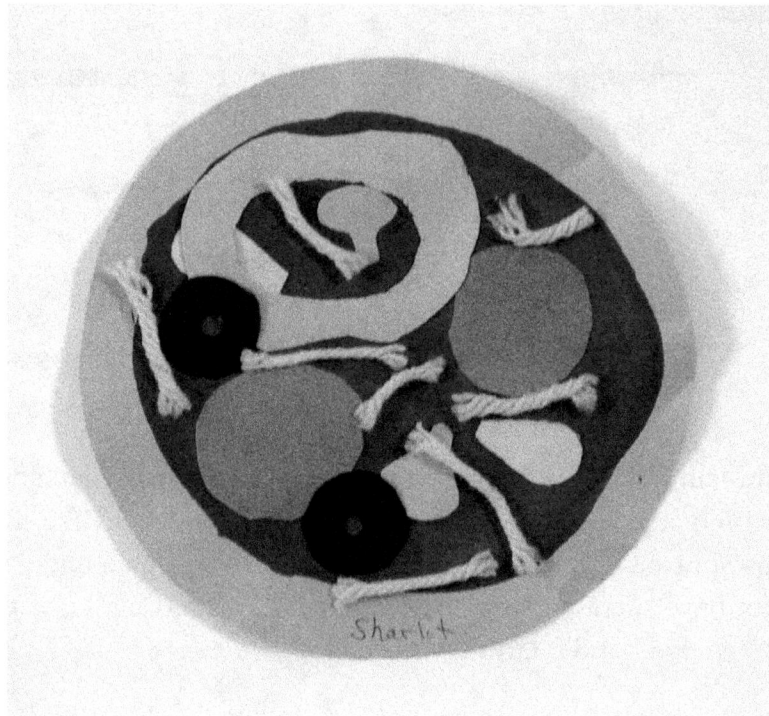

## Muffin

Draw a muffin on a sheet of 8 ½" by 11" piece of paper, making it as large as the paper. Then glue it on a piece of poster board. Cut the muffin out and use it as a template to make about 5 muffin tracers.

Have children use the tracers to trace on white paper with a pencil. They can cut it out or leave it that way. Next, set out the watercolors for them to paint their muffin.

## Grain Collage

Use a sliced bread pattern to tell how to make large bread slice shapes on 9" by 12" paper. Place shape on top of paper and trace it out or copy it on a copy machine. Then staple the printed or traced pattern on top of at least 6 pieces of plain paper. Then cut out enough for each child to have one. Children will glue grains onto the piece of bread. You could use wheat, corn, rice, and different grain cereals. Talk with children about the different grains and how they are used while they are working at the table.

## Apron

Draw the outline of a baker's apron on white paper. Children will decorate the apron with dot markers, stamps with stamp pad, markers and/or crayons. Children will also write their names on the apron where the rectangle on the apron is located. See sample to the right.

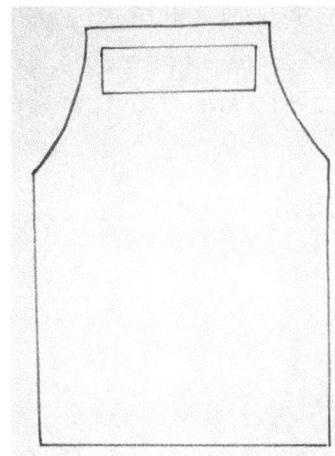

## Corn

Use a corn cob pattern outline to copy or to make for each child. Then children will glue popped popcorn inside the outline of the cob. Teacher will write across the bottom - I got too hot to keep today! Now I'm Popcorn.

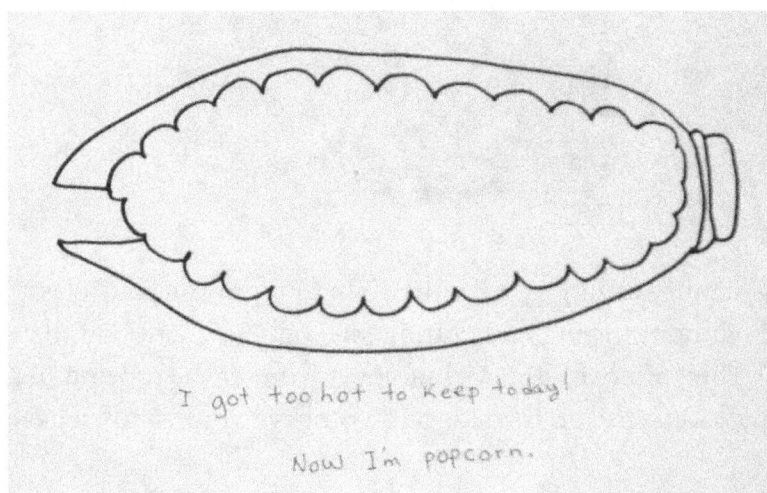

I got too hot to keep today!

Now I'm popcorn.

Children will use a lot of small finger muscles to glue their popped popcorn on this project.

## LANGUAGE AND LITERACY

### Silly Sandwich

You can use this at the language table or as a group activity in your class.

Use the image below to make pattern for silly sandwich. Draw a slice of bread on card stock and cut it out. Then trace several of them onto brown paper. You will need a front and a back for each sandwich. Next, using the same pattern, trace it onto white paper. Two slices will fit on a piece of regular 8 ½ by 11 white copy paper. Put the traced sheets on top of six or more pieces on plain white paper. Then staple around outside of pattern on each side. Now cut them out and you will have enough pages for 3 sandwiches.

Continue in this manner until you have the right amount for your class. This is a faster way to cut things without tracing and cutting so long. Now write on the top brown slice "Silly Sandwich". Then put two slices (white sheets) under the top and next add a bottom brown slice. Staple two times on the side and you have your sandwiches prepared.

Have on hand pictures of different sandwiches. Children will identify what they see on the sandwiches. You can use pictures from advertisements and magazines for examples. Then children will discuss what they like on their sandwiches. Next, give each child a prepared pretend sandwich and ask them to open their sandwiches and draw the things that they like on the white pages. When they are finished, have them tell you what the pictures are and write the words by their pictures.

This gives them the opportunity to express themselves and increase their vocabulary.

### Letter "S"

Draw large letter "S", like the one below and trace and cut one for each child in your class. Cook enough spaghetti for your size of class. Don't rinse off, you want it to be sticky.

Talk to the children about the sound the letter "S" makes. Have them look at the letter and make the "S" sound several times. Then show the children the spaghetti and have them sound out the word spaghetti several times. Ask them what letter it is. Now put the cooked spaghetti out and have them place the spaghetti anyway they want to on their letter S. Ask them when they are finished what their letter is and what sound it makes. You can also ask them it they can think of any words that begin with that "S" sound besides the word spaghetti.

### Breads

Have these supplies on hand: white bread, wheat bread, multi-grain bread, French bread, and raisin bread.

Give each child a piece of each kind of the breads. Talk about the things that are similar and different between each slice. For example you could talk about the colors of the breads, how they smell, how they look and how they taste. Expressive language helps them to increase their thinking and self expression. There are no right or wrong answers only different opinions.

### Creative Pasta

Prepare and provide macaroni, colored pasta, rigatoni (large tube pasta), glue, crayons and paper. Children will create a person or animal. Then the children will describe what they made, what it likes to do, what it eats, where it lives and any other information they want to tell you about it. Next write down the words that the children tell about their creation.

## Wordless Book

Use the wordless book, <u>Pancakes for Breakfast</u> by Tomie DePaola. Children will look at the pictures in the book page by page and they will take turns telling what is happening on each page of the book. Encourage them to say at least a three word sentence. If they only use two words encourage them to say more. Example - Child says, "a bowl". Then you say, "You see a bowl that is?" Child says, "I see a bowl that is yellow." You say, "You see a bowl that is yellow and?" Keep repeating what they said and have them add to it. This will help them learn to be expressive and use their thinking skills to really look at the pictures and know what the story is about. You could pick any wordless book at your library to do this activity or use a picture book, but don't read the words.

## Prepositions

Teacher will use plastic small farm animals and small cups for this activity. Each child will pick a farm animal and be given a cup at the start of this activity. Then the children will be directed to put their animal in the cup and then to take it out of the cup. Children will follow directions together. They will also be directed to say the animal (example like their pig) is in the cup and then the pig is out of the cup. Continue using different prepositions like under the cup and over the cup, behind the cup and in front of the cup. After going through them several times have the children take turns telling others where to put their animal while they also put their animal where they say it is going.

**CREATIVE ARTS**

## Creative Arts

Cut out large food shapes such as muffins and circles (for pizza). Have different colors of poster paint mixed with a little dish detergent for them to paint these shapes. Also, have large pieces of plain rectangle sheets for them to paint other things of their choosing.

Then put the easel out with the paint cups full and have crayons on the easel trays too, so that they can use them together for small or large details in their pictures.

Another shape you could cut out to be used another day would be to use the apron pattern listed earlier under fine motor. Clip the apron patterns on the easel along with dot markers so that they can make patterns on the aprons to decorate them. Also cut out large chef hats. Encourage them to write their names on their pictures or have you help them do it.

## SENSORY

Place flour in the sensory table with 2 or 3 mini muffin tins, 3 or 4 small bread pans, 4 or 5 spoons for stirring, 1 or 2 flour sifters, and 2 or 3 bowls.

Place wheat in the table with small collections of farm animals, craft sticks to make fences and small plastic trees too. Farm animals can often be found in the dollar stores.

Place a hand grain grinder in the table with a supply of wheat and bowls to put the flour in once it has been ground. If you have a grinder that needs to be screwed to a surface to work, use it on a wood table. Be sure and show them how it works and stay close by or have other adults watch children to make sure that they don't put their fingers inside grinder. They won't go fast because of the hard work involved in grinding wheat so keep encouraging them that they can do it. This is a good muscle builder. They will be excited to make their own flour.

Cook up some spaghetti and color it with food coloring or leave it plain. Now place it in the table with scissors and bowls. Children will cut and cut into small pieces. This is a good activity to help them practice cutting.

## DRAMATIC PLAY & SOCIAL DEVELOPMENT

Have a supply of plaid flannel shirts, red bandana scarves, old cowboy boots and hats along with stick ponies for a fun farmer and/or cowboy/cowgirl experience. You can find many of these items at thrift stores and from parents in your class. Stick ponies can be made using patterns found at your local material shop.

## SCIENCE

Use small baby food jars or other clear small containers to put an assortment of grains in for children to view with magnifying glasses. Some of the grains available are wheat, buck wheat, rice, corn, millet and oat meal. These grains and others can we found in health food stores by the pound and stores that specialize in food storage and preparation or mixers and grinders.

Also put with them pictures of how grain look when they are growing. Look in the children's section of non-fiction books in your library for them.

## GROSS MOTOR SKILLS

### Bread Basket

Make necklaces from yarn and hang pictures of various things made from grains like muffins, donuts, hamburger bun, hot dog bun, cookie, bread, biscuit, bagel and crescents on them. Watch in the grocery ads for these pictures. Be sure and laminate them so that they will last better. Once you have found a picture you like, make copies of it so you can use them for the necklaces. You will need at least two of the same picture for the necklaces so that there are matching ones.

Children will set in a large circle on chairs and wear their necklaces. Then the teacher will explain the rules of the game. Everyone will take turns saying the name of the grain product they are wearing. Then when she calls out the name of a grain product, the person wearing that necklace must change places with another person that is wearing the same necklace. For example, teacher says biscuit. The two children wearing biscuit necklaces must hurry and exchange places. The teacher will keep calling out different grain products, but when she calls out bread basket everyone must change places at the same time.

### Popcorn Hop

The teacher will set out a trail made from popped corn. It will be located outdoors. The children will be told that they must start the game where a large taped "X" is on the ground. Then they must follow the trail by hopping. When the teacher calls out a different skill such as giant steps, the children must stop hopping and start taking giant steps while following the popcorn trail. Play continues until they reach the end of the trail. There will be a bag with a popcorn ball for each student. They will sit on the grass and eat them. The birds can have the remaining pieces.

# FIELD TRIP IDEAS

### Grocery Store

Call or stop by a grocery store in your area and find the bakery department. Make arrangements for a tour of that department. Children can look at the many things made from grains and see how they are made and packaged. Most stores are more than happy to accommodate this request and will even let the children sample some products.

### Bakery Shop or Bread Shop

Arrange a visit to a local bakery or bread shop. Children can observe the large mixers and ovens used there along with how they are made. They can often observe a worker decorating a cake or other process. Talk about what they do there and how they do it.

### Farm

Arrange for a trip to see how the grains grow and see all the big machinery that is used there to harvest them.

### Rolling Mill

Arrange to see a rolling mill to see how the grain is process into flour.

# Health, Doctor & Dentist

## GROUP ACTIVITIES/CIRCLE TIME

### MUSIC AND MOVEMENT

"Brush Your Teeth" from "Singable Songs for the Very Young" CD or tape by Raffi. Children enjoy using their index finger as a pretend toothbrush, whenever the song says you brush your teeth. They also hold up the correct number of fingers when the tape says the time. This is a short simple song, so they learn it fast and they can sing it without the tape soon.

"Popcorn" from "We All Live Together" Vol. 2 CD or tape by Greg Scelsa. Children have fun acting out this song while being reminded that popcorn is a good snack.

"Head Shoulders, Knees and Toes" Traditional

Sing this traditional song while touching parts of body mentioned. You can add more names of the body when they have learned these. Be sure and start out singing the song slowly as they learn it and then sing a little faster.

Head, Shoulders, Knees and Toes

Head, shoul-ders, knees and toes,

knees and toes,

knees and toes

Head, shoul-ders, knees and toes,

eyes, ears, mouth and nose.

"Beanbag Boogie", from "Kids in Motion" CD by Greg & Steve. Children will follow directions of where to put their beanbag and what movement to do with their beanbag. Bean bags can be made using small squares of material. Sew around three sides of the square. Then turn the bag inside out and put uncooked beans or for a softer bag use rice to fill bag partly full. Next turn raw edges inside and sew opening closed.

"Apples and Bananas" from "Five Little Monkeys" CD of Traditional songs. In this song children sing the first verse by singing with the CD. Then for the other verses of the song the words apples, bananas and eat will change by adding a new vowel to the first of the words: eat- ate, apples - aypuls and bananas-banaynays. Listen and change words with the CD. This is a fun way to talk about health foods and learn vowel sounds.

"Dr. Jane" from "Touched by a Song" CD by Miss Jackie

"Wash Your Hands", from "Touched by a Song" CD by Miss Jackie

"The Dentist Is Your Smiles Best Friend" from "Touched by a Song" CD by Miss Jackie

"The Doctor" tape from Macmillan Sing & Learn Program by Newbridge Communications, Inc. Children will follow the directions for movement on the tape or CD.

"9-1-1" tape from Macmillan Sing & Learn Program by Newbridge Communications, Inc. Children will pretend to have a phone and use their finger to push the 9-1-1 numbers with the tape. They will also pretend to pick up the receiver by pointing the thumb and pinky finger out while tucking the remaining fingers in. This song helps them to learn when a problem is an emergency and how to call for help.

"Healthy Body" tape from Macmillan Sing & Learn Program by Newbridge Communications, Inc. A song that children will listen to and learn about their body.

"Just say Ouch" tape from Macmillan Sing & Learn Program by Newbridge Communications, Inc. Children will pretend to do all the actions in the song and learn how to keep safe.

"Washcloth Squares" tape from Macmillan Sing & Learn Program by Newbridge Communications, Inc. Teacher will give each child a napkin or small paper towel to be their washcloth. In this song and children will pretend to wash the different parts of their body that the song says. This will be a fun reminder to wash their bodies all over.

"Three Times a Day" from Macmillan Sing & Learn Program by Newbridge Communications, Inc. Children will act out this song and be reminded to brush their teeth three times a day.

"The Breakfast Song" from Macmillan Sing & Learn Program by Newbridge Communications, Inc. In this song the children will act out fixing lots of health foods for breakfast and learn the importance of eating breakfast each day.

"Mr. Weatherman" from Macmillan Sing & Learn Program by Newbridge Communications, Inc. Children act out this song and learn how to dress for the weather.

"Sleeping Time" from Macmillan Sing & Learn Program by Newbridge Communications, Inc. Children will learn the importance of resting each night through pretending to do the things on the tape.

"Mulberry Bush" Traditional song. You can find tune of the traditional verses in the book Heritage Songster by Leon and Lynn Dallin page 257. Instead of singing verses about how we wash our clothes and hang them out to dry, use verses that say this is the way we wash our face, wash our hands, brush our teeth, brush or comb out hair, take a shower or bath.

"Early to Bed" This traditional song can be found in the book Heritage Songster by Leon and Lynn Dallin Page 256. Instead of saying, "Makes a man health-y" say "Makes a child health-y." This is a simple and short song that children can learn quickly to reinforce getting enough rest as night.

## LANGUAGE AND LITERACY

This book list will help you to select books about the dentist, doctor, and keeping healthy that children have enjoyed in my classes.

Arthur's Eyes by Marc Brown, Little, Brown and Company 1979.

Visit the Doctor by M. J. Carr, Scholastic INC. 1993.

Doctor De Soto by William Steig, Scholastic INC. 1982.

My Tooth Is Loose! By Susan Hood, Reader's Digest Children's Books 1999.

A Visit to the Dentist by Eleanor Fremont, Scholastic INC. 2002.

The Berenstain Bears Visit the Dentist by Stan & Jan Berenstain, Random House New York, 1981.

Just Going to the Dentist by Mercer Mayer, A Golden Book New York, 1990.

I Know Why I Brush My Teeth by Kate Rowan, Scholastic INC. 1999.

Bearobics by Vic Oarker, Emily Bolam, Scholastic INC. 1996.

Albert the Running Bear's Exercise Book by Barbara Isenberg & Marjorie Jaffe, Ticknor & Field A Houghton Mifflin Company, 1984.

I Hate to Be Sick! By Aamir Lee Bermiss, Scholastic INC.2004.

Elmo Says Achoo! by Sarah Albee, Random House New York, 2000.

Germs! Germs! Germs! By Bobbi Katz, Scholastic INC. 1996.

The Missing Tooth by Mary Packard, Scholastic INC. 2002.

Franklin and the Tooth Fairy by Paulette Bourgeois, Brenda Clark, Scholastic INC. 1996.

Going to the Doctor by Fred Rogers, Scholastic INC. 1995.

After reading these books, be sure and ask children about the topic like, "Have you been to the dentist before? What was it like? Why do we wash our hands?"

Be sure and include activities at the circle like using a pail, water, soap and paper towel to demonstrate the proper way to wash their hands and dry them.

Also use a large toothbrush to demonstrate the correct way to brush their teeth. Make large teeth by cutting the bottom of small water bottles off and staple them together to form and half circle of pretend teeth. Then with the bottoms up, spray paint them white. See example below.

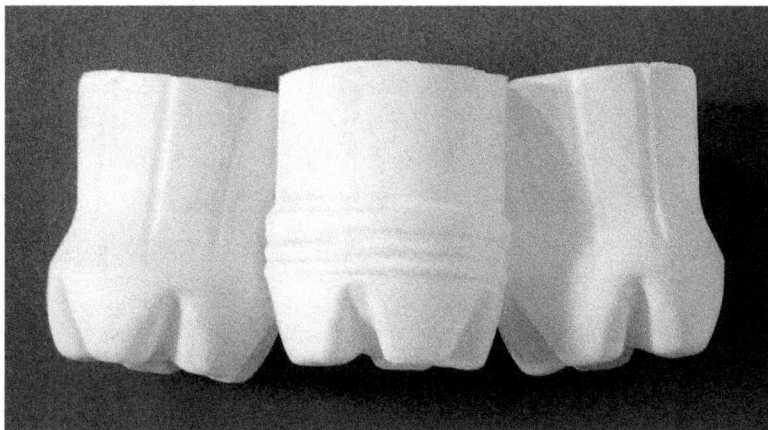

Now demonstrate brushing them by making small circle strokes on the tops and sides of the teeth with the large toothbrush. Another fun way to teach about germs would be to take a balloon and with a hole punch, punch twenty of more punch outs and put them inside the balloon. Now blow the balloon up with air and tie the end closed.

When the children have talked about the book, Elmo Says Achoo! get the balloon out and a pin. Next put the balloon by your mouth and pretend to sneeze, while sticking the pin in the inflated balloon. Tell the children that the small circles represent the germs that go everywhere when you sneeze. Explain to them the importance of covering your mouth and nose with a tissue or by placing their arm across their nose and mouth when they feel a sneeze coming on.

## SMALL GROUP ACTIVITIES/TABLE TIMES

### MATH & COGNITIVE

**Tooth Size Activity**

Draw four teeth and make each tooth bigger than the last one. Place these teeth on heavy paper and trace around them. Now you can use these as a quick way to make more teeth for the children to use.

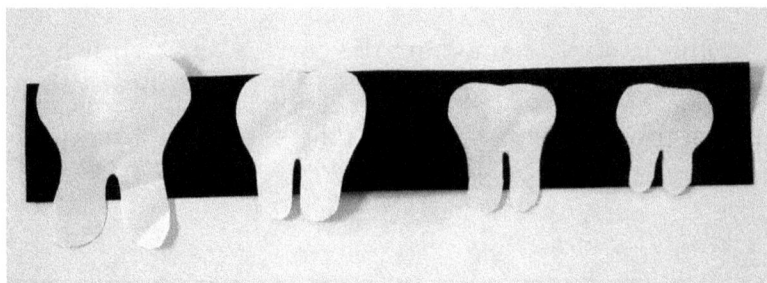

Staple five pieces of copy paper together and trace on the top sheet the four sized pattern as many times as you can fit on a page. Now cut the teeth around the traced lines. Make sure that you make a set for each child in your class. Next, use long pieces of colored construction paper and cut them about 2 ½" to 3" wide to make long stripes for each to mount their teeth on.

Tell the children to arrange their set of teeth from biggest to smallest and then to glue them in that order onto their strip of paper. See example below.

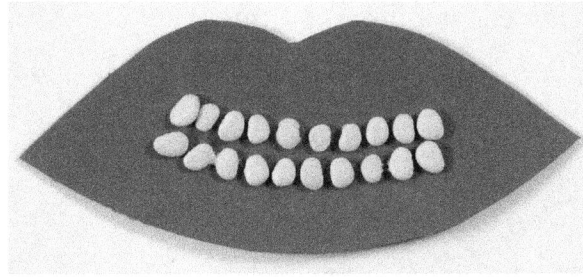

## Teeth Counting

Trace and cut large lips from red construction paper for each child in class. Children are given small lima beans and glue. Tell children to glue the teeth inside their lip cutout. Have them count how many teeth they used. Then write the number of teeth for the child or help the child write the number. Before children leave the table, have them count their bean teeth one more time while touching the beans one at a time. See example below.

## Toothbrush Game

Use a piece of poster board to make this game board. Decide on the size you will use for the amount of children at your table. Then make a curving line across the board and color it and add some stickers for decoration. See example of game board.

Next label one end start and the other end finish. Cut plain index cards to size wanted and write questions you want children to review from circle time discussion on each card. Some examples are: When do we brush our teeth? How do we brush our teeth? What is floss? How do we use floss and why do we use it? What foods help our teeth? What foods aren't good too eat often? What kinds of drinks are good for us and what kinds should we have only sometimes? Prepare a few cards that say move back one space and several that say move ahead 2 or 3 spaces and mix them into the pile of cards.

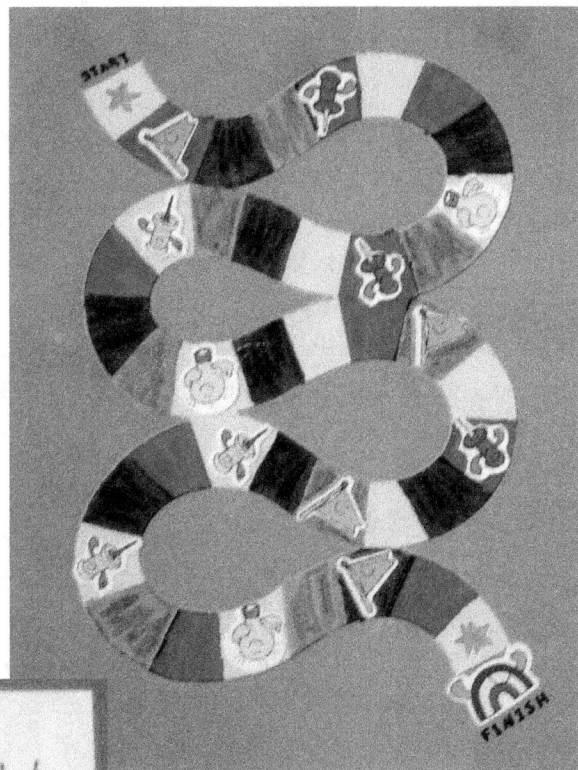

Assign each question a number amount like 1 through 5 moves.

Laminate the cards. Cut them out and put them in a stack. Use colorful buttons or other small items for markers. Make sure that the children will be able to identify their own marker. Now you're ready to play!

Children will take turns drawing a card. Then teacher will read the question on the card and that child will try to answer the question correctly. Help a little if needed. If the child answers it or is helped and answers it, let the child move the number of points found of the card. Continue having the children take turns drawing cards until everyone makes it to the finish. Let the children who finish first with their questions, help those that need a little help. At the end of the game give each child a sticker for a reward.

## Healthy Body Game

Use same game board as the "toothbrush game", but use different cards for this game. Example of questions: How much rest do we need? Why do we need to rest? What is exercise? Why do we need exercise? Name at least two ways to exercise. Why should we drink water each day? How much should we drink each day? Why should we keep our bodies clean? What are two ways we can keep our bodies clean?

Mix in cards that say go back one space and several that say go ahead 2 or 3 spaces as in the "toothbrush game". Play using fruit o's, buttons or other small objects. Children will take turns drawing a card. Then teacher will read the question on the card and that child will try to answer the question correctly. Help a little if needed. If the child answers it or is helped and answers it, let the child move the number of points found of the card. Continue having the children take turn drawing cards until everyone makes it to the finish. Let the children who finish first with their questions, help those that need a little help. At the end of the game give each child a good snack for a reward such as pieces of an apple.

## Loose Tooth Game

Draw a horseshoe shape on pink card stock. Make it about 2 inches wide. Then glue it on a white or red rectangle shape. Make two cards for each child in your small group. Then on the pink horseshoe shape place ten one inch white squares evenly around it. Glue them down and laminate each group of two together. This will represent their top and bottom teeth. Use small white marshmallows or lima beans to represent teeth.

Buy a large die with dots instead of numbers. If you can't find one, make it by cutting a small child's school milk carton into a square and cover it with four squares of poster paper. Then make dots from one to six on it and tape them securely around it.

Game play: Tell the children that they will pretend that this is their mouth full of teeth. Tell them that children have ten teeth on the top and ten teeth on the bottom, but as they get older they will start losing their baby teeth and getting new big ones. Have children put one of the pretend teeth on every square of the mouth. In this game they will take turns rolling the die and counting the number of dots on the die. Then they will remove that number of teeth. Play continues until all of the teeth are gone.

These games take a little extra work, but they can be used many times during the year as reminders of dental or physical health. The children will also like to use them more than once during this theme. It's fun for them to repeat the games so that they can say the correct answers that they have learned.

## Graphing

1.  Have each child count how many teeth that they have lost. At top of paper or a chalk board make columns and then write numerals 1, 2, 3, 4 across the top of the columns. Now ask each child to tell you how many missing teeth that they each have. Then have them make an "X" under the column heading that matches that amount. Continue with the next child and continues until all the children have had a turn. Then with the children count and total each columns amounts. Ask the children which is the largest number, the least number and/or same amount. Also use the terms most, fewest and tied to expand their vocabulary.

2.  Have three different kinds of tooth paste for the children to have a very small taste of. Use foil or plastic wrap to place very small amounts of the different types of toothpaste on. It would be helpful to use ones that have different colors and flavors. Use q-tips for the tasting that can be used once and thrown away after using. Prepare columns as above (only need 3 columns).

Illustrate the color of the tooth paste over the column or use numbers on the paste foil to match the different flavors. Now have each child taste the three different types of paste and vote for the one that they think taste the best by marking an "X" under their favorite. When all the children have voted have the children count and total each column. Ask the children which is the largest number, the least number and/or same amount. Also use the terms most, fewest and tied as mentioned in the previous graphing activity.

Choose either of the graphing activities to use with the children and you could do the other one later in the year when reviewing teeth care

## FINE MOTOR SKILLS

### Alligator Teeth

Ask parents to collect the gray paper egg cartons for this. Cut each carton cup apart until there is one cup for each child. Make shapes of heads on card stock paper for tracers that the children will use. See example. Have white poster paint, old toothbrushes, glue, stapler, markers, large plastic wiggle eyes, green construction paper, and child scissors ready for use.

Children will use tracers of head shape to trace two heads for a top and bottom on the green paper. Then they will cut them out. They will also cut up and down in a zigzag across the top, front side of their egg making sharp teeth. Next paint the gray teeth with the white paint using the old tooth brushes. Let it dry while children decorate the top head with a marker by drawing on nose circles, dots for bumps and eyebrows. Now they will either glue eyes under eyebrows or draw them on with the marker.

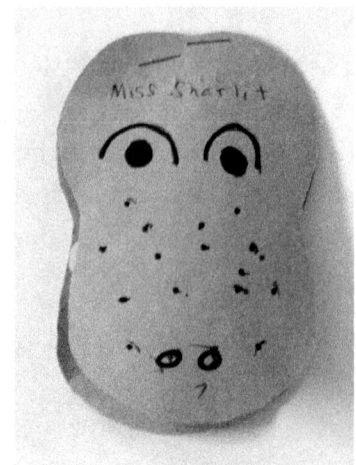

Next they will glue to the top of the green head the egg carton teeth with the teeth pointing down by place the glue on the flat cup circle bottom. Keep it upside down while it dries. When it dries, staple the two head parts together at the opposite end of the mouth. The alligator will remind them to keep their teeth white.

### Tooth

Teacher makes large tooth patterns for children to use to trace around. Children trace around pattern and then cut out the tooth and make a face on tooth. Remind children to take good care of their teeth.

### Tooth Collage

Use a large pattern of a tooth and either have children cut their tooth out or the teacher cuts one large tooth for each child in the class. Then children find pictures of healthy food to cut and glue onto their large tooth. You can find food pictures in magazines or in grocery store advertisements.

## Toothbrush

Use a piece of construction paper to make a large handle for a pretend toothbrush. Cut construction paper lengthwise about 4 inches wide. Then fold the paper length wise down the middle. This makes the handle. Now have the children fold another piece of white copy paper in half and then in half again. Staple along the long folded edge. Cut off edge of short folded edge. Now open handle and place staple edges between pieces of handle. Then place white part at the end of one of the handle ends. Glue in place on both sides of the white paper. This makes the brush part. Now children will use scissors to cut in straight lines from free end of paper to colored handle. Children will continue to cut up to the handle in lines about ½ inches apart until they reach the end of the white paper. Children write their own names on their toothbrush handle. Display these brushes on the walls.

## Watercolor

Put the paints out with plain pieces of white paper and tell the children to paint a picture of something that shows how they will take care of their teeth. Examples - them or their family brushing their teeth in the mornings, pictures of healthy foods they will eat for snacks and etc.

## Cavity

Prepare a large tooth with a black cavity drawn on it. Children are given toothpaste mixed with a little white glue, a craft stick and pieces of white paper. Children will tear the white paper to fit the cavity. Then they will fix the cavity using the "special" glue with their craft to fix their pretend tooth cavity.

## Doctor Bag

Provide double long construction papers. Children will begin their activity by folding the paper in half and caressing it down the middle so it resembles only one piece of construction paper. Then place a simple card stock pattern over it to create bag shape with the fold side on the bottom. Children will use a piece of chalk to trace shape, so they can see, it's done on black paper. Then children will cut it out the top and sides. Now they will staple the sides closed to form their bag. Use this bag with the language activity "Simple First Aid".

52

## LANGUAGE AND LITERACY

**Match the Teeth**

Make simple teeth patterns of white card stock and cut out at least 16 teeth. Then draw matching eyes, noses and smiles on a pair. Continue by making more pairs with it pair looking different. Example see below of eyes open closed, frown or smile. Laminate them for durability.

Place the cards on the table with the faces showing. Then tell the children to examine the teeth carefully to find pairs that are just the same. Play begins by children taking turns finding matching pairs. After matching teeth children will tell how the teeth are alike making sure to talk about the differences if they choose two that are not alike. Play continues until all of the pairs have been matched up.

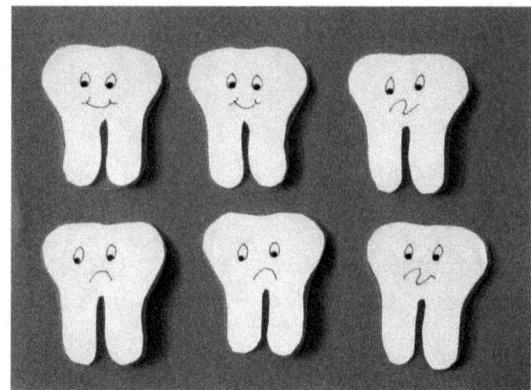

**Healthy Foods**

Make two sack puppets. Use lunch sacks and glue a large head on each of the bags. The heads should have a large open smiling mouth on one and a large frowning open mouth on the other one. The mouth should be large enough to place pictures of food into their mouths. Then find pictures of food from magazines that will fit through the puppets mouth and laminate them also. Make sure that you collect lots of good foods and some foods that children should only eat occasionally such as candy and cake.

Children play by taking turns holding the puppet with a happy face or a frown on it. The children also take turns choosing a food picture. They will tell what the names of their foods are and then feed them to the correct puppet. The child holding the puppet will tell the other child if that is a happy food to eat for healthy teeth or one that makes them unhappy by eating it too often. Play continues until everyone has had a turn doing each thing or until they tire of doing it.

**Doll Prepositions**

Obtain 5 or 6 dolls and 5 or 6 unused toothbrushes. Tell the children not to put these brushes in their mouths. They will pretend using these toothbrushes by placing them in various places. Tell them to listen carefully and place the brush where the teacher says.

Example put the tooth brush behind the doll, in front of the doll, in the dolls mouth, on the dolls foot, over the dolls head and etc.

Children will say the position of the toothbrush while placing the toothbrush in the correction positions. Then the teacher will let the children take turns telling the rest where to put their toothbrush. The child giving the directions will also put their brush in the correct position. Play continues until everyone has had a turn being the leader.

## Object Order Game

Buy at the store a few dental tools such as a small mirror that goes in your mouth, floss, a toothbrush, a dental pick, and a tooth x-ray film. Also have a small tray in which to put the objects and a small towel to cover the objects from view.

To play, show the children the objects one at a time and have them tell you what they know about each object. Then tell them that you will place three of the object on the tray in a special order and that they need to remember the order of the objects.

Next teacher tells children to close their eyes while you mix up the order of the objects and when you tell them to open them they will place the objects back in the correct order they were it at the start. Use the towel to hide the objects from their view because they usually peek. Then mix them up and have children open their eyes. Next take turns having them put the object in the correct order after mixing them each time.

## Simple First Aid

Teacher will obtain these items: small zip-lock bag, bandages, first aid towels in individual wraps, and vinyl/latex disposable gloves.

Begin by asking children if they have had a fall before and how it felt when it happened. Show the children the first aid items. Take turns asking them what each items is and how it is used. Have a discussion of ways that they could use each item to help them self or someone in their family. Tell them that they can use the gloves to keep blood from getting on their hands and from getting germs on someone else. Now have them place the items into their zip-lock bag. If they made the doctor bag from the fine motor activity have them place the bag into it to take home.

## Exercise Head Band

Get material with stripes on it and cut them into about 2 – 3 inch wide and 10-12 inch long pieces, however long enough they need to be to encircle their head. You'll also need permanent markers.

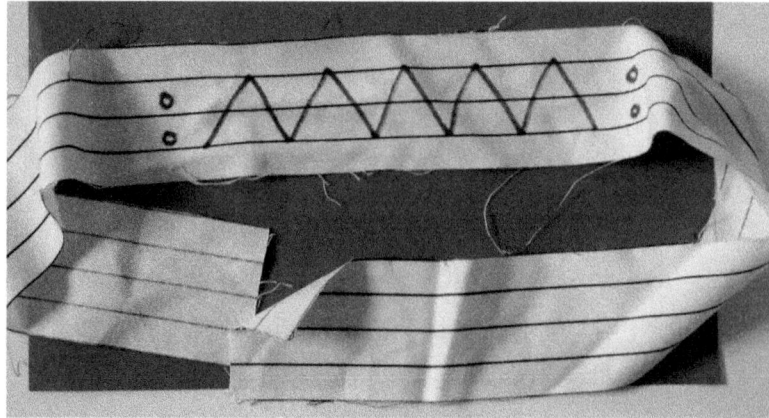

Have a discussion on being physically fit or read parts of the book, <u>Albert the Running Bear's Exercise Book</u> by Barbara Isenberg & Marjorie Jaffe or <u>Bearobics</u> by Vic Oarker.

Then they will make head bands using the stripe material. Let them draw between the stripes or draw lines to connect the lines. Have them write their names on it and tie it around their foreheads before they go outside to try a few of the exercises. See picture.

## 911

Make balloon numerals of the emergency number 911 on pieces of construction paper or print them on card stock. Talk about what is an emergency and when you should call 911. Make sure they know not to call unless a big person can't help them because they are not conscience or if they are left alone. Also explain that you never call it for any other reason. Use a pretend phone so they can practice dialing it. Then have them glue beans or other small craft items inside the numeral balloons. See example.

# FREE TIME

## CREATIVE ARTS

Cut out large teeth shapes for the children to paint on. Clip the shapes to the easels. You can have them use paint brushes or provide sponges to dip into the paint. Another different idea would be to use toothbrushes to dip in different colors so that they can make different designs on the teeth.

Another fun thing to do is to use the large teeth shapes to collage on. Provide beans, pasta, craft items, or small paper shapes to glue on the teeth. You could also include markers for them to draw their own creations on the teeth - like teeth germs.

## SENSORY

Put warm water in the sensory tub with foam teeth and toothbrushes. You could also use plastic animals with teeth like alligators for the children to play with and brush their teeth.

Use baby dolls in the sensory table with pails of sudsy water and wash cloths to clean the dolls.

Use shaving cream on trays in the sensory table with small squeegee to clean the trays off so they can make new designs in the shaving cream.

## DRAMATIC PLAY & SOCIAL DEVELOPMENT

Use large blue shirts to represent doctor, vet, or dentist clothing. Get these from thrift shops or from parents. Buy a few toy doctor kits and add bandages, elastic wraps and some stuffed animals along with dolls to doctor up. Provide play phones, magazines for the waiting area with chairs and an office sign along with an eye chart. They will enjoy this make believe play. Children need to know that they take turns with the items and if it's very popular that it will be up for as long as it's still popular so that they can have lots of turns.

## SCIENCE

Teacher cooks several hard boiled eggs and shows them before placing them in bowls with root beer. The eggs represent out teeth and the things that we eat and drink can stain them. After they are stained provide toothbrushes with toothpaste near by in an empty bowl so they can brush them to clean away the stains.

## GROSS MOTOR SKILLS

### Exercise to Music

Use Walt Disney Mousersize tape or any music with a happy steady beat to exercise. They can touch their toes, hop on one foot and then the other, swing their arms in circles or any other exercise. Teacher has the children follow what she/he does. They must watch closely because you keep changing the exercises.

### Doctor, Doctor, Patient

This game is played like "Duck, Duck Goose". Children sit in a circle and one person is chosen to be "it". The player that is "it" goes around the circle saying, "doctor, doctor" while touching them on the head softly. This continues until he/she reaches the child that he/she wants to be chased by. Then the child says to that child, "doctor, doctor, patient" while touching their head softly. Then that child gets up and runs behind the person that is it. The child that is "it" runs around the circle until he/she reaches the place where the one touched sat. He hurries and sits there. The one chasseing him/her now becomes "it" and starts moving around the circle again saying, "doctor, doctor." Remind the children to choose a new person each time so that everyone has a turn. Play continues until your time is gone or everyone has had a turn. If some children didn't get a turn write their names down and make sure that they are the first ones to have a turn when there is time to play again.

## FIELD TRIP IDEAS

Arrange to go on a field trip to a dentist office or if you have a training school for dental assistants try there. They often have more time to spend with you and the children. Ask before hand if the children will be able to sit in the chair that goes up and down and see the different tools used besides the x-ray machine and some old x-rays.

Have the children prepare before going there by reading books about dentist and thinking of questions they would like to ask. Write down their questions and children's names with them to take with you. They often forget what they wanted to know when they get there, so this can help them.

Another thing to do before going it to make thank you cards to take with you or learn a special song to sing to them when they leave the office. Teacher could use a piece of poster board folded down the middle and make A large tooth for the front of the card. Then children could draw inside of it and write their names. Take photos of the children in the chair or standing by things in the office.

When you return from the field trip or the next day if you are out of time, have children do drawings about what they saw on individual papers with their names on them. Then have them dictate to you what their drawings represent. Write their words on their pages and put them into a binder along with the developed photos of the trip. Make sure and read this book to the whole class and place it where they can look at it on their own.

58

# Thanksgiving

## GROUP ACTIVITIES/CIRCLE TIME

### MUSIC AND MOVEMENT

"The Pilgrims and the Indians" from "I Have a Song For You About Seasons and Holidays" tape by Janeen Brady - Brite Music Enterprises, Inc.

"Sharing" from "I Have a Song For You About People and Nature" tape by Janeen Brady Brite - Music Enterprises, Inc.

"My Brother and I" from "I Have a Song For You About People and Nature" tape by Janeen Brady Brite - Music Enterprises, Inc.

"She's My Sister" from "I Have a Song For You About People and Nature" tape by Janeen Brady- Brite Music Enterprises, Inc.

"We Are Going to Grandma's House" from "I Have a Song For You About People and Nature" tape by Janeen Brady - Brite Music Enterprises, Inc.

"I Love My Grandpa" from "I Have a Song For You About People and Nature" tape by Janeen Brady - Brite Music Enterprises, Inc.

"I Love You" from "Barney's Favorites Vol. 1 tape Columbia House

"My Family's Just Right for Me" from "Barney's Favorites Vol. 1 tape Columbia House

"The Sister Song" from "Barney's Favorites Vol. 1 tape Columbia House

"The Sharing Song" from "Singable Songs for the Very Young" tape by Raffi

"We All Live Together" from "We All Live Together" Vol. 1 CD by Greg Scelsa

"The World is a Rainbow" from "We All Live Together" Vol. 2 CD by Greg Scelsa This song helps children be aware of all the many people of the earth and that we many have different colors of skin, but we all have something to give each other when we live in harmony.

"May There Always Be Sunshine" from "10 Carrot Diamond" CD by Charlotte Diamond This is a great song to have children be involved in, so they can express all the things that they always want to be on the earth. Children add to the song what they always want to have.

"The Turkey Stroll" from Macmillan Sing & Learn Program by Newbridge Communications, Inc. on CD or tape. Children will act like turkeys in this song in song and movement.

"The Thanksgiving Song" from Macmillan Sing & Learn Program by Newbridge Communications, Inc. Children will be reminded of the many things to be thankful while singing this song.

"Over the River and Through the Wood" from "Heritage Songster" Music Book by Leon and Lynn Dallin Wm. C. Brown Company Publishers.

"Thanksgiving Song" from "Heritage Songster" Music Book by Leon and Lynn Dallin Wm. C. Brown Company Publishers.

"Ten Little Indians" from "Heritage Songster" Music Book by Leon and Lynn Dallin Wm. C. Brown Company Publishers.

"Ha Ha Turkey in the Straw" from "Piggyback Songs Compiled" by Jean Warren Book by Totline Press

"A Thanksgiving Song" from "Piggyback Songs" Compiled by Jean Warren Book by Totline Press

"Our Grace" from "Piggyback Songs Compiled by Jean Warren Book by Totline Press

"Let Us Give Thanks" from "More Piggyback Songs" Compiled by Jean Warren Book by Totline Press

"Smells Like Thanksgiving" from "More Piggyback Songs" Compiled by Jean Warren Book by Totline Press

"Mr. Turkey" from "More Piggyback Songs" Compiled by Jean Warren Book by Totline Press

A song that I made up for our class to say thank you to people for helping us goes like this:

Thank You Song

> Thank you, thank you, thank you!
>
> Thank you, thank you, thank you!
>
> Thank you, thank you, very much!
>
> Cha, Cha, Cha!

Sing the first 2 lines in the same key and sing the 3rd and 4th lines in a higher key. When you sing the Cha, Cha, Cha! part have the children bend both arm at the elbow with hands in fist while swinging them together from side to side.

All the songs by "totline" are easy to sing because they use simple turns from nursery rhymes for the tunes and the songs are short. Children enjoy singing them and they learn them fast.

There are many songs listed about families because that is the main thing that children readily think of when asked – "What are you thankful for?"

## LANGUAGE AND LITERACY

Raggedy Ann A Thank You, Please, and I Love You Book by Norah Smaridge, Western Publishing 1972. Raggedy Ann and Andy teach good manners.

Big Sister & Little Sister by Charlotte Zolotow, Harper & Row 1966. The story of a little sister learning to know what it's like to be a big sister and loving each other.

Monster Manners by Joanna Cole, Scholastic Inc. 1985. Rosie's family learns that it helps to have good manners.

Giving Thanks by Rita Walsh, Troll Communications L.L.C. 1997.

Winnie the Pooh's Thanksgiving by Bruce Talkington, Disney Press 1995.

Giving Thanks a Native American Good Morning Message by Chief Jake Swamp, Scholastic Inc. 1995.

Franklin's Thanksgiving by Paulette Bourgeois and Brenda Clark, Scholastic Inc. 2001.

'Twas the Night Before Thanksgiving by Dav Pilkey, Scholastic Inc. 1990.

Feeling Thankful by Shelly Rotner and Sheila Kelly, Ed.D., Scholastic Inc. 2001.

Cranberry Thanksgiving by Wende and Harry Devlin, Parents' Magazine Press 1971. This story teaches you can't judge other's by appearances and includes the recipe for the Grandmother's famous cranberry bread from the story.

Froggy Eats Out by Jonathan London, Scholastic Inc. 2001.

A Turkey For Thanksgiving by Eve Bunting, Scholastic Inc. 1991.

Thanksgiving Day by Anne Rockwell, Scholastic Inc. 1999.

Over the River and Through the Wood by Lydia Maria Child, Scholastic Inc. 1998.

Clifford's Thanksgiving Visit by Norman Bridwell, Scholastic Inc. 1993.

During and after reading a book be sure and ask open ended questions like - "What did this page mean to you? How do you feel about that? What was the most interesting part to you? What do you like to do at Thanksgiving time?"

After reading one of the books about being thankful, ask each child to name one thing that they are thankful to have. Write each answer on a paper turkey feather. Put all the feathers behind a large turkey that is located on your wall. These will serve as a reminder to be thankful for all their many blessings.

## SMALL GROUP ACTIVITIES/TABLE TIMES

## MATH AND COGNITIVE

### Turkey Match

Make copies of small turkeys and then cut out various shapes to glue on the turkey's body. Make pairs of each turkey shape, and then laminate them. Children will take turns looking at all the turkeys with shapes and make matches with the two turkeys that are the same. Next, they will tell the shape name of the turkeys they found that match each other. Play will continue with the next child making a match and telling the name of the shape they matched. Continue with children taking turns until all the pairs have been found and matched.

## Table Setting

Buy or make paper place mats for each child in the class. If made, use wall paper rectangles. You can get these from a wallpaper store. Ask for a discontinued sample book, if you can't get it donated to you, ask how much you could buy one for. Usually the cost will be little or free when you explain that it's for a preschool.

On a regular place mat draw circles where the plate and glass should be located and trace around or draw the placing of the silverware. Have the children watch as you place the items on the correct circle and tracings. Then children will take turns placing the items on your mat. Also, explain where the napkin goes. When they have finished taking turns, give each child a paper plate (or use the plate they made at the fine motor table), paper cup, paper napkin and a place setting of plastic silverware. Tell each child to set their setting on their paper place mat in the correct place and glue them to the mat. They will take these examples home so that they can help set the table correctly.

## Turkey Number Cards

Use small turkey pictures that you have copied and write numerals from 1-10 on them. Have the children take turns finding the turkeys with the numerals you say in the turkey. Call the numbers in a mixed up order and then have them help you place the turkey numbers in correct order from 1-10. Then take turns with a child and have him/her call the numbers for the child to find and then have the child ask the other children to help him/her arrange the numerals in correct order. Continue to play, but stop playing before they lose interest, so they will want to play again another day.

## Turkey Number Match

Use the same pictures of turkeys from for the "Turkey number game", but you will need to put numerals on them in pairs instead of the shapes. You may want to laminate them so that you can use them many times. When playing with the children, turn the turkey cards face up and spread them on the table. Children will take turns finding two numerals that match. When they make a match they will say the numeral name and then set the pairs in front of them. The next child will take a turn matching the turkey numeral cards and saying their name. Play continues until all of the numeral cards have been matched. Other children can help the children name the numerals if needed. Next have children put the numerals in order from 1-10 and say the numbers as they are placed in order.

## Horn of Plenty

Draw or buy a picture of a horn of plenty. Then copy them to make four or five cards. These will be the game card base. You will need to cut a card stock square to be placed on top of the picture. The square will need to have six columns on it. In the left column, write numerals from 1-5 by starting at the top of the column and going down. The columns will be made into squares by drawing lines evenly across the diagonal columns. Now laminate cards. Use cubes or other small counting objects like dollar store bags of glass gems with flat sides. Children will place one token in the first column by the numeral one and two gems by the numeral 2 in the next two columns one in each column. They will continue through the rest of the numerals until they have completed all 5 numerals and all five columns by numbers are completed correctly. The columns will look like stairs when completed. See example.

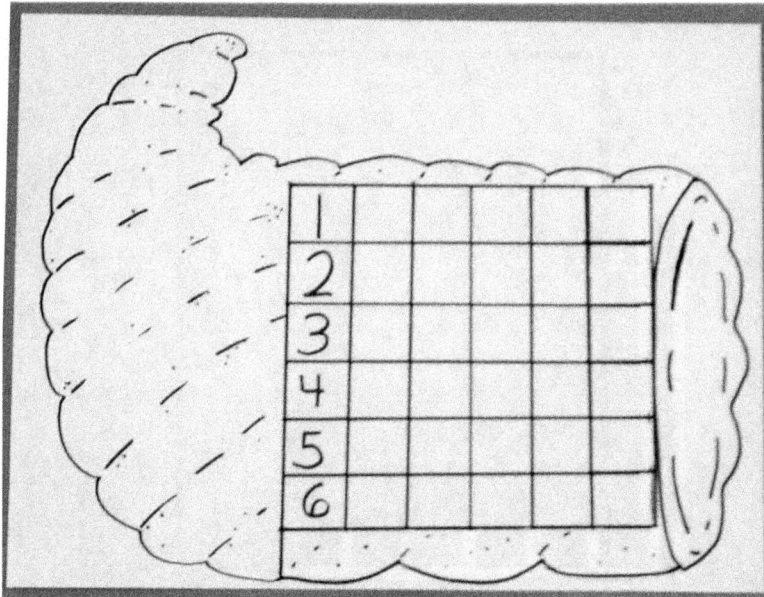

## Indian Corn

Buy four ears of Indian corn at the store. Buy them in four different sizes or break them into four different sizes. Children will take turns arranging the corn from biggest to shortest. If they can't do four of them correctly have them do three. The two middle ones seem to confuse them, but they will learn to do it with practice. Children will take turns doing this, but if you want it to go faster buy more sets of four corns.

## Feather Game

Make a long strip of material for each child to use with enough feathers for each to child to have from a bag of feathers. Teacher will also need to use squares of paper with numerals written on them from 1 to 5 written several times each. Help children put a headband on their heads. Then children will take turns drawing a number card. They will count that many feathers to match their numeral and place them behind their head band. If they can't read the number, have dots on the back of each number card that they can count to determine the numeral. Play will continue until each child has had at least four turns. You can have the children keep their head bands or leave them at the table to reuse again.

## Turkey Feather Game

Prepare a turkey body pattern from brown construction paper and have the children glue it onto a white piece of construction paper. Make sure that there is one for each child in your class. Use a die with numbers/dots 1-6 on it. Children will take turns rolling the die and counting the number of dots on it. Then they will get that many feathers from a bowl on the table and glue them onto their turkey. Then the next child will roll die and count out that number of feathers to glue on his/her card. Play continues until children have had 3 or 4 turns each. See example of body below.

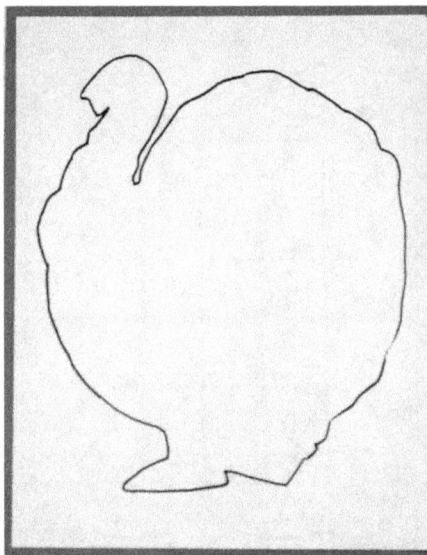

## FINE MOTOR SKILLS

## Decorative Plate

Supply large plastic lids from cool whip containers or from number 10 cans for the children to use as tracers. After they have traced their circle they will cut it out and decorate it by drawing on it or by gluing small craft items such as sequins on it. This plate will be used with the cognitive activity of table setting.

## Turkey

Use simple turkey shape such as the example below. This shape can be copied onto the page or it can be cut out from colored paper and glued on the page by you or the children. When the turkey body has been put of the center of a blank page, children will be ready to add the feathers. Children will create their feathers by drawing lines out from the turkey body. Then teacher will have foam trays with mixed poster paint in different colors in them. Children will use their pointing or index finger to dip into the paint and then make a print of their finger next to their straight lines. They will continue to make prints up and down each of their lines to create the turkey's feathers. Have a pail with warm dish soap waiting for them in which to wash off the paint so they don't have to touch the handles on the sink until most of the paint is off their hands.

## Turkey Hand Card

Teacher will have white paper ready for the Children to fold. They will fold it in half once. The top fold of the papers will become the front of the card. Children will put their hand on the front of the paper to trace around their hand with the fingers open and the thumb away from the fingers. The thumb will become the turkey head and the out stretched fingers will become the feathers. After the tracing, the children will use markers or crayons to color the feathers and to draw the legs and feet on. Have plastic wiggle eyes for them to glue on the head. Later at the language table they will dictate to the teacher what they want to say and the teacher will write their words inside their card. The children will write their own name on their card.

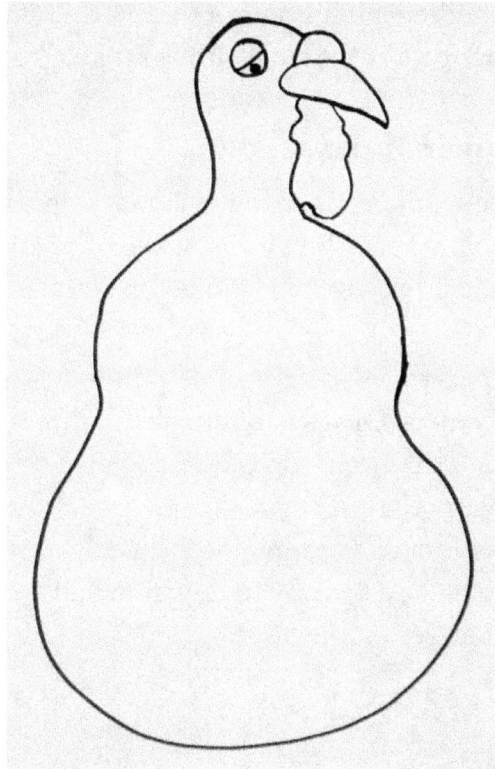

## Indian Corn Print

Put out more Indian corn. Long pieces of water color paper should be set out for them to use along with mixed poster paint. Fall colors of paint work best for this activity. Use large foam trays to hold the paint. You can buy these from a bakery store. Children will roll their ear of corn into the paint and when make a print of their work by rolling it again on their water color paper.

## Family Stick Puppets

Teacher will trace around small lids, such as yogurt lids to create heads. Then cut out five or six heads for each child in your class. If you know how many people are in each family, then you could cut out the exact number of head for each child. Provide markers, masking tape and craft sticks for use with the puppets.

Children will draw faces on each head to represent each members of their household. Next help them tape the head to the stick. When the puppets are complete have the children place them into a plastic bag with their name on it. Children will use these puppets at the small group language table.

## Apple Turkeys

You will need the following: one apple for each child, a box of tooth picks, a bag of mini colored marshmallows, a bag of regular sized marshmallows, a bag of small wiggle eyes and a package of chenille pipe cleaners cut into short one inch pieces.

Teacher will demonstrate putting toothpicks into the back, top side of the apple to form feathers. On each toothpick put three or four mini marshmallows. Then place a toothpick into the front, top of the apple and place one large marshmallow on it to represent the head. Use the small chenille pieces for feet by placing three together in a "V" shape at the bottom of the apple on each side at the bottom. Use an additional chenille pipe cleaner to make a beck by folding it in half and pressing it into the marshmallow. Last of all, glue the eyes on the head.

# LANGUAGE AND LITERACY

## Family Stick Puppets

Use the stick puppets made at the fine motor small group table for this activity. Children will take turns introducing their puppets to the children at the table. They will tell others the puppets names and how they are related. Example - This is Nancy Smith. She is my mom.

Then they will tell their brother and sister names and how old they are or if they don't know their ages have them tell if she/he is older or younger that they are. They could also tell what they like to eat or do together. Save the puppets for use on another day.

The next time you get the puppets out, have the children take turns using the puppets to show how their family does one or more things. Example - Share things, help each other, plays together, uses kind words, uses good manners and etc.

## Thankful Pictures

Children will use crayons or markers to draw pictures of what they are thankful for. Then they will dictate to the teacher what they want to tell about the things that they are thankful for in their picture. Teacher will write their words on the picture.

### Feather on the Turkey

Make a turkey body out of colored construction paper, but leave off the tail feathers. Make feathers out of different colors of construction paper cut them out individually. Laminate turkey body and feathers to make it durable. Children will take turns picking a feather and telling the color name of the feather. Then they will place the feather on the turkey body. The next child will take their turn and play will continue as before until all the feathers are gone.

### What's Missing?

Collect pictures of various objects from magazine such as tables, chairs, bikes, toys, and etc. Then cut off a part of the picture so it is missing a part. Example missing a chair leg or a wheel on a bike. Mount them on poster board or just laminate them.

Children at your table will take turns looking at a picture and telling what's missing from the picture. This activity helps them learn visual perception and expressive language.

### Hide the Turkey

Teacher will provide a cup and a small plastic turkey. Teacher will move the turkey to various positions like in the cup and ask a child where the turkey is now. Child should us the words "it's in the cup." The goal is to have children use the correct position words. Play continues by asking another child where the turkey is when you have moved the turkey under the cup. Continue asking one child at a time where the turkey is after moving the turkey to various places. The places to move the turkey could be: over, under, between (2 cups), in front of, behind, beside out, in, on top, and make it go around the cup. This helps children learn prepositional words and their meanings. Another day when they have some of the wording correct have them have them take turns hiding the turkey and asking other children to tell where the turkey it now.

### Manner Keys

Draw the shape of a simple key. Then make an additional four more keys on a piece of paper. That makes five keys in all. Write these manner words on the keys: Sorry, Please, Thank you, Excuse me and May I help you?

Next make a copy of the key page for each child. Have scissors for the children to cut out their keys and a chenille pipe cleaner for each of them. Tell them that you want to talk to them about some important keys that will help them get along better. Then show them the keys one at a time and ask them why and when they would use that key. Continue showing and talking about each key one at a time. Then ask the children to cut out their keys. Have a chenille pipe cleaner for them to fasten all their keys together to take home.

## CREATIVE ARTS

**FREE TIME**

Cut out various shapes using the paper cutter and die cut math shapes. This would also be a good project to have parent volunteers do to help you. After your supply is ready, place the shapes in small containers at the easel. Provide glue bottles and markers at the easel also. Now clip paper to the top of the easel for the children to glue and create on. Tell them that they may make anything that they want, but be sure and have a few examples of things that have been glue together to make a few things so that they get the idea of how to do it.

As the week goes along add other items to the easel such as chenille pipe cleaners and foam packing peanut and craft sticks so that they can make their pictures three dimensional.

## SENSORY

Use un-popped popcorn in the sensory table with empty small and large bottles, funnels and scoops. The laundry detergent scoops can be saved and washed to be used in the sensory table.

Another idea would be to use wild bird seed in the sensory table with small plastic farm animals. Put in craft sticks to make fences for the animals too.

# DRAMATIC PLAY & SOCIAL DEVELOPMENT

Put old fashioned grandma and grandpa type clothes with shoe and hats in a prop box for children to dress up in. Make sure that there is a mirror close by so that they can see them selves. Add accessories such as jewelry and ties and some books that show pictures of how people used to dress. Play older days dance music too like waltzes.

# SCIENCE

Put books about turkeys on the science table. Also put samples of the food they eat and make a tape of the sounds they make that children can play to listen to their sounds. If a turkey farm is near by you could record their sounds and ask for some feather to display. Also display Indian corn and various types of fall squashes. Have some of them cut open so that they can see their seeds.

# GROSS MOTOR SKILLS

## Sack Race

Teacher obtains empty potato sacks from a farm supply store or buys pillow cases from a thrift store for this fun activity. Divide the children into two groups to make two teams with one sack or case for each group. Place half of each team facing each other a predetermined space a part. Use tape or a hose to mark how far they must hop to reach the rest of their team members. Then demonstrate how to put both feet into the case and then to hop while holding each side of the top tightly. Child on each team will receive a sack or case and when the signal to go is said they will hop to their team facing them. When they reach their team they will get out of the case/sack and the first member on that side will get in and hop to the other side. The player that has already hopped will go to the back of line that he hoped to and sit down. The new players will hop to the team members facing them and give their sack to player in front. Then she/he will go to the back of that line and sit down. Play continues until all members of the teams have sat down.

## Parachute Turkey

Find some Thanksgiving inflatable decorations to use with the parachute. These can be found at party stores. If you can't find any you can purchase foam balls and draw on them with permanent markers. Use three or four balls or objects of various sizes. If you don/t have a parachute use a large sheet. You can buy these at thrift stores. Children will gather around the parachute or sheet and pull it tight. Put the object on top of the parachute/sheet and have the children raise the parachute up and down while holding the sides tightly. Then have them shake it. Children will raise and lower it again. This time try and knock the decorations off the chute.

## Bounce the Ball

Children are still working on hand-eye coordination so this activity will help them develop it. Divide the class into two groups to make two teams. Place half of each team facing each other about three feet apart. Use tape or a hose to mark how far they must stand apart. Place a picture of a turkey in the middle of each group and have the children face each other so that they can bounce the balls to each other. Children use the picture in the center of their team as a target to bounce their ball off. Next the child on the other side of the line catches the ball and bounces it off the target to the same person that threw the ball. Then they both go to the back of the line and sit down. The next two team members bounce their balls to each other as before and then sit down at the back of the line. Play continues until all children have had a turn.

## FIELD TRIP IDEAS

Make arrangements to visit a turkey farm. Children will be able to watch the turkeys and see how they live and what they eat. If a turkey farm isn't available try a chicken farm. They may let you see how they collect the eggs to sell and what they eat. A small regular farm may also be an option. Some of them have a few chickens and a turkey or two to observe.

# Where To Get What You Need

There are many different places to get what you need. If you use your imagination, many items can be substituted for what you have on hand, can get for free, etc. For example, you may have an abundance of baby food jars from a family toddler. You can easily convert these to be part of a project. Teaching is also about being resourceful. Have family, friends, students and yourself save:

- Baby food jars

- Toilet paper rolls

- Paper towel rolls

- Scraps of material

- Extra tile

- Extra pieces from home improvement projects

- Coffee cans

- Oatmeal containers

- 2 liter bottles

- Cereal boxes

- Egg carton

- Milk jugs

- Salt containers

- Anything you can think of to be re-purposed for a learning tool

Other places to get materials include:

- Home improvement stores (Lowes or Home Depot)

- Dollar Stores

- Educational Supply Stores

- Grocery Store

- Party Supply Store

- Online Resources:

  — Oriental Trading Company: www.orientaltrading.com

  — http://www.etacuisenaire.com